Parenting with Self-Compassion

12 Ways to Improve Your Parenting, While Being Kind to Yourself

Jen Ferris, PhD

Platypus Publishing

The cartoon *My Wife and My Mother-in-Law* in Chapter 8 was drawn by W.E. Hill in 1915.

Publisher: Platypus Publishing
Paperback ISBN: 978-1-968253-29-5
Cover design and illustrations: Jessica Bell
Edit: Kirsten Rees
Edit and interior design: Liz Pond

Connect with the author:

Instagram: @drjenferris
Facebook: @drjenferris
Threads: @drjenferris
TikTok: @dr.jen.ferris
Bluesky: drjenferris.bsky.social
Website: DrJenFerris.com
Email: DrJenFerris@gmail.com

To Justin, I wouldn't have wanted to go through this crazy ride with anyone but you. Thank you for giving me a beautiful place to write and for your honesty and support.

To K and J, for illuminating my world. This book would not exist if it were not for you.

*This book is for the parents who are just
trying to get through the day.
May it help make things a little easier.*

Contents

Medical Disclaimer

All of the content here is for informational purposes only and does not constitute medical advice.

I have a PhD in family psychology, but I am not a therapist. Although I strive to give accurate information, what is presented here is not a substitute for professional therapeutic care.

Possible Trigger Warning

At the end of Chapter 3 there is a brief discussion about childhood trauma. You are welcome to skim or even skip that chapter completely.

Chapter 1

Parenting is Tough, but Self-Compassion Helps

"If you're completely exhausted and don't know how you're going to keep giving this much of yourself day after day, you're probably a good parent."

Bunmi Laditan

I placed my infant in my husband's arms, locked myself in our tiny bathroom, and sank onto the closed toilet seat. Alone, I bawled my eyes out.

Overwhelmed, I had no hope that things would ever get better. It felt like our baby cried non-stop. I was exhausted from feeding her every two hours and getting no solid sleep. My hormones were up and down like a roller coaster and I wanted to scream and break things.

"How was this my life? Where had things gone so wrong?" I got myself together and went back out.

"Are you okay?" my husband asked.

"No, not really." I didn't care if he knew—in fact, I needed him to know. I needed help from him, and from anyone and everyone who would give it to me. I was a new mother after all.

I had high expectations of myself as a parent. I was a child development professor with an MA in child development and a PhD in family psychology, and I had worked with children, including infants. I had all this education and experience.

But, at that moment, I felt like a complete failure.

It's hard and expensive to have a baby. Add in all the hormones, sleep deprivation, and physical changes, and it's no wonder that new parents, especially single parents, feel exhausted and overloaded.

There are moments when we want to scream, cry, or both. Like when your baby spits up on your last clean shirt or there's exploding diarrhea going up and out of your baby's clothes. There are also moments when your child snuggles in close, smiles at you, takes their first steps, says "Mama" or "Dada," and gives you a big bear hug just because. There are high highs and low lows.

Parenting is hard, but like Glennon Doyle says, "We can do hard things."[1]

I loved my newborn but I couldn't believe how insanely difficult things were. When I was home with my baby then I wasn't working and felt I was falling behind. But when I was at work I was thinking about my baby and not truly present. Nothing felt good enough.

Year one as a first-time parent was brutal and I was tough on myself. I thought, "What's wrong with me? Why isn't this easier?"

If you've ever felt like this, you are not alone.

Self-compassion helped me when nothing else did.

Compassion means to suffer with someone. When you have compassion for a friend, you can tell that they're suffering and you want to help them.

According to Drs. Kristin Neff[2] and Christopher K. Germer,[3] leaders in the field, self-compassion is doing the same thing for yourself, seeing that you're having a tough time, and wanting to make it better.

Instead of criticizing yourself for the things you may see as personal failings, you give yourself kindness, warmth, and understanding. You know that just like everyone else, you're human and deserving of love and care.

Note: "Self-compassion" is in the title, but this book does not claim to be the definitive title on the subject. This is a book for parents. It's filled with ideas to make parenting easier and less full of conflict and stress, as well as ways to raise great children—all while being kind to yourself. I want parents to be gentler with themselves and with their kids.

If you would like more details on self-compassion, please feel free to look at the Notes section.

Benefits in Parenting

When we're compassionate with ourselves, it's easier to be patient and present with our children. By being kind to ourselves in the difficult parenting moments, we can stay calmer and have less conflict, stress, and tension in the home and in life.

Instead of reacting on impulse when we're frustrated, we can be curious and flexible, responding to our kids in a way that builds a better relationship.

As we admit to our mistakes and treat ourselves gently, our kids see that the world will not end if they make a mistake. They learn to be kind to themselves too.

It's a Challenge to Have Self-Compassion

It can be hard to have compassion and empathy for ourselves. It's often easier to be warm and forgiving toward others than toward yourself.

The good news is, self-compassion is a learnable skill, like a muscle you strengthen by using it. While it can take time, with practice you can develop more self-compassion. But why does self-compassion even matter?

People with high levels of self-compassion are

- happier and healthier
- less critical of themselves
- more self-confident
- more productive and resilient.

They have

- improved self-esteem
- less loneliness and more social connectedness
- better relationships
- less disordered eating
- less stress
- less depression and anxiety.[4]

Ways to Build Your Self-Compassion

Talk to yourself like you would a good friend

What would you tell your best friend if they were feeling upset? You might say, "I'm so sorry that you're going through this right now. What can I do to help?" or "It sounds really hard right now. It would be for anyone. I'm here for you."

If it's something you'd suggest to your friend, like more self-care and rest, then you can give yourself permission to do it too.

Remember you're not alone

It can feel like you're the only one in the world going through something, but the truth is there are so many parents out there having the same thoughts and feelings. This sense of shared humanity helps us feel more connected to others, like we're all in this together.

Ask yourself, "What do I need right now?"

Maybe you need some rest, a shower, a walk, or to talk to a good friend, a therapist, or coach.

As I was writing this chapter, I felt unwell, but I tried to push through. I finally had to stop and ask myself, "What do I need right now?" I responded with, "I need to rest. I'm sick." It was disappointing, but the world did not end.

My hope is that you can figure out what you need and get it.

Put a hand on your heart

As you might do when you feel something deeply, putting your hand on your heart is a simple way to feel less anxiety and more compassion. This practice can lower your heart rate and stress levels, and can make you feel calmer and more secure.[5]

For me, it reminds me to take a deep breath when I may be holding it without realizing it.

Give yourself a compliment

"It's been hard to get up lately, but I did it, and I got everyone to school and work on time. I'm proud of myself."

"My child was upset and made a scene. I stayed calm, got us out of there, and talked with them about it. I like how I handled it. I'm a good parent."

"I made a nice meal tonight."

"I was kind to a stranger at the coffee house in front of my kids."

How many times do you find yourself doing something right as a parent yet not giving yourself credit? Notice when this happens and give yourself the pat on the back that you deserve.

Now go a step further. What are some of your qualities that you appreciate? See if you can think of three or four things that you like.

I'll go first: I have curly hair, brown eyes, and I can do cartwheels.

It's normal to think of the superficial things first. Can you go deeper? What's good about your personality or who you are?

For me, I'm kind to others and good with kids and animals.

Now, you go. Be honest. I know there are many good qualities within you. Are you smart? Funny? Giving? Honest? Able to read people well? Good at math or computer games?

Dr. Pooja Lakshmin[6] writes about her personal journey with IVF. She realized that she "could not control the outcome, but what I could control was how I treated myself—mentally and physically."

Practice mindfulness

Mindfulness means paying attention to the present moment without judgment. You aren't going over the past or worrying about the future; instead, you're curious about what is happening right now.[7]

Being mindful leads to less stress, anxiety, and depression. People feel calmer, have a greater sense of well-being, and are more resilient.

And when you're mindful, your self-compassion increases. When you're aware of the pain that you feel in the present moment, you can have compassion for yourself for feeling that way.

Mindfulness improves your parenting because it helps you calm your emotions and be less reactive in times of stress.

It's like you're outside of yourself noticing that you're about to react to your child in a way that you don't want. Instead of yelling, you choose to take some deep breaths, and you realize that it's okay if you're a couple minutes late to a playdate. They will understand. It's not the end of the world.

Parents who practice mindfulness are more satisfied with their parenting skills and their interactions with their kids. They have children who are less aggressive, have improved social skills, and get along better with their siblings.[8] To find mindful parents and classes you can go to Community of Mindful Parenting.

Meditate

There are different kinds of meditation including breath, senses, walking, body scan, progressive muscle relaxation (PMR), grounding, and loving kindness meditations.

There is no wrong way to meditate.

If you're focusing on the breath, when you notice your mind start to wander, which is completely normal, just return to the breath. "Oh, that's thinking." And then back to the meditation.

See what comes up without judging it. It's a skill that takes practice. If you keep doing it, even for just a few minutes, you're doing great. The hardest part is starting. I found it helpful to attend a class and have a teacher.

There are so many benefits to meditation including: (1) less stress, anger, chronic pain, anxiety, and depression, (2) lower blood pressure, (3) improved mental focus, sleep, impulse control, and well-being, and (4) a boosted immune system.

If you're curious, there are many apps for breathing exercises and guided meditations. You can check out Insight Timer, Calm, Headspace, Balance, and Ten Percent Happier. Take a look and see what feels like a good fit for you.

There is a great talk by Elizabeth Gilbert on Insight Timer, called "Facing Fear with Compassion", that helped get me through the pandemic. For more information and examples, see the bonus chapter in this book on meditation.

Practice gratitude

At night before you fall asleep, think of three things that happened to you that day that you're grateful for. If you can only think of one, start there. Keep a gratitude journal if you are able.

Did your child say thank you, take their first steps, enjoy a long nap, or bring you a flower for no reason?

Was a friend or family member there for you? Perhaps a barista or cashier was funny or nice today. Did the dog greet you with a wagging tail? Are you thankful for that delicious hot tea or coffee? You might appreciate the sunshine, birds chirping sweetly, or that you and your family are healthy.

Focusing on the good in our lives brings about relaxation, kindness, and connection. We tend to be happier and more optimistic, and less stressed and depressed. It's also easier to deal with negative events when they come up.

Forgive yourself

Making mistakes and learning from them is a part of growth. When you forgive yourself for the things that you've done in the past, you can let go of guilt and resentment, and have more empathy for yourself.

Everyone makes mistakes and feels pain
sometimes. This is part of being human.

When you forgive yourself for a mistake and learn from it, it's a good lesson for your children to see too.

Work on self-improvement

Self-improvement can include books, classes, support groups, or finding a good therapist or coach.

Notice when you lack compassion for yourself. Is it often around work problems, communication issues with your partner, or trouble with the kids?

This can tell you when you need positive self-talk and self-compassion the most. Then, when these situations come up again, you can move toward positive change.

It can be hard to develop self-compassion on your own, especially if it wasn't modeled for you as a child. Therapy with a safe, supportive counselor can help you notice self-critical thoughts and feelings, and figure out how to build self-kindness instead.

See Chapter 4 for ways to find a good therapist, and the Center for Mindful Self-Compassion for courses on self-compassion.

When I first got pregnant, I went to the bookstore and picked up some pregnancy books. I had to stop reading those books because they freaked me out. They went into detail about all the possible things that could go wrong, when all I wanted was to stay calm and relaxed for me and my baby. I looked at other parenting books, but they were too long, scientific, and tough to read.

My goal here is to give you a short, easy-to-read book on parenting for infants through to pre-teens, which has ideas you can go back to as your kids get older.

While the focus is on how you can be kind to yourself, you will also get suggestions on ways to communicate with and discipline your children, including neurodivergent kids. There will be parenting tips, like picking and choosing your battles, ways to offer choices, seeing things from your child's perspective, and how to take a parent time-out that actually works. You'll learn how to meet other parents, ask for help, and get technology recommendations, such as when to give your child a phone, and much more.

Parenting can be incredibly difficult, but I want to help make it easier and give you the support and compassion you deserve.

Let's get rid of the blame and shame, and
focus on being gentle with ourselves.

Sit and Think: Is there an area in which you could use more self-compassion?

Action: Try one or two of the ways to build self-compassion. What happened? How did it feel?

Share: Share your experiences with self-compassion on your socials with #ParentingWithSelfCompassion or at DrJenFerrie.com.

To get better as a parent, it helps to let go of the idea of being "perfect."

Chapter 2

Letting Go of the Idea of Perfection

"You don't ever have to balance it completely. [Parenthood] is a constant struggle of a little more time there, a little more time here, and feeling a little bit guilty all the time."

Halle Berry

One afternoon, my children had finished their homework and they were fighting; one wanted to play a board game and the other wanted to be left alone. They were shouting at each other, their loud voices contagious. I yelled, "Enough!" and ordered them both, "Go to your rooms!"

I didn't like that I had raised my voice. A few minutes later, I went to talk to each of them to get their side of what had happened. Then we all got together and figured out what each of us could do better in the future, including me.

It was important to me that I rarely raised my voice with the kids. So when my husband and I noticed that it was happening too often for our liking, I talked to a therapist. I got tools I could use to calm down before it got to the point of yelling, to respond better in the moment. Was I perfect? No, but with work and effort I got much better.

An Epidemic of Guilt

American parents feel guilty about 23 times a week.[1] They feel bad about losing their temper, missing their kids' activities, and not being home enough to play with their kids, help with homework, and make home-cooked meals. Some parents feel like they aren't doing a good enough job when they let their kids have too much screen time and processed foods.

Maybe your parents were great, and you feel pressure to make them proud, and to be as involved and as patient as they were with you.

Even with all of this guilt, we tend to parent better than we think we do.[2] According to recent studies, moms and dads are spending more time with their kids now than they did in the past.[3] Children won't remember that there wasn't a fancy, five-course meal, but they will remember that you sat down, ate together, and talked about your day. We're never going to be perfect as parents, and that's okay.

There are No Perfect Parents

I thought I could be a "perfect" mom—the one who hand-makes all her own organic baby foods, cooks wonderful family meals from scratch, works outside of the home, keeps a beautifully clean house, and has company over.

Ha! I do cook sometimes. I have worked outside of the home. I have had company over. And my house has been clean. But not all at the same time. Are you kidding me?

Perfect parents do not exist. We're all human and we all make mistakes. The important thing is that we don't keep making the same mistakes over and over again; that we learn from them and get better.

We might look at these happy, put-together families on TV and social media and think, "Why can't my family be more like that?"

Here's a picture I posted online after having my first baby. Great, right?

Now I'm being vulnerable here, so please be kind, but here is a picture of my actual home life that I *did not* post on social media.

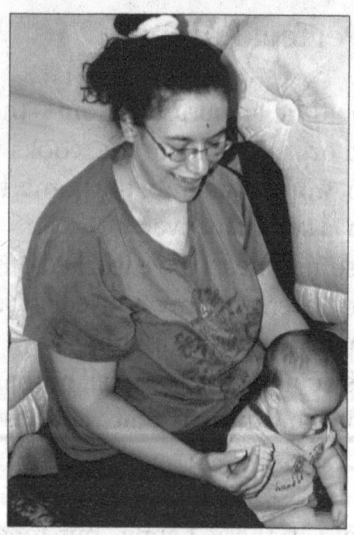

Well, I guess I am sort of posting it here, whoops! But you can see why I didn't, right? I've got the messy bun going on, the acne, and the moderately clean T-shirt.

How people look online can be very different from reality. Seventy-five percent of parents say they feel pressure to look and be a certain way, and that the pressure comes from family, friends, and social media.[4]

And it's not just parents who feel this pressure. The belief that you can't have any flaws has been increasing in young people too.[5] In a study of more than 40,000 American, Canadian, and British college students, they found that perfectionism increased between 1989 and 2016.[6] Recently, 24,000 Canadian high school students were surveyed and more than half of them said that they felt this pressure.[7]

But what is perfectionism?

Perfectionism

Perfectionism is when you demand "an extremely high or even flawless level of performance, in excess of what is required by the situation."[8]

It's wanting to look, feel, and be free of any imperfection, to try to gain approval and acceptance.[9] Perfectionists set unrealistically high expectations and are critical of themselves and others.

But what's so wrong with trying to be the "best version" of yourself? Isn't it good to have high standards? Well, there can be downsides. When you're scared to make mistakes, you may procrastinate, give up too soon, or avoid trying new things.[10]

Perfectionists have

- increased stress
- more sleep problems.[11]

They're at a higher risk for

- anxiety and depression
- obsessive-compulsive disorder (OCD)
- bipolar disorder

- eating disorders
- substance abuse
- suicide.[12]

So how do we deal with this?

Cognitive behavioral therapy (CBT) has been found to be helpful for perfectionists by letting them see and slowly change their harsh beliefs about themselves and learn new ways of thinking.[13]

Perfectionists may work on setting small, realistic goals and telling themselves that it's okay and normal to make mistakes.[14] It can be helpful if they're able to switch to positive self-talk, learn mindfulness, and practice self-compassion.[15]

Stop "Shoulding" All Over Yourself

Are you telling yourself that you "should" be a perfect mom or dad? One who never gets tired and bakes cookies all day instead of buying them at the store? If you're a single parent, do you feel like you "should" be able to do it all? Do you think you "should" find more time, be calmer, have a cleaner house, go to bed earlier, and drink less coffee? Blasphemy.

When we hear ourselves think in "shoulds," it's our negative self-talk telling us that we aren't good enough.[16]

Sure, there will be some things that you have to do whether you want to or not, like going to work and feeding your kids.

But if you have a few free, precious moments...

Sit and Think: Ask yourself: "Am I doing this because I want to or because I think I should be doing it?" "What do I actually want to do with this time?"

 Action: Do what you want to do at least once a day. If you truly want to lie down and rest, then doing the dishes or cleaning up can probably wait. Remember the advice that Phyllis Diller gave in her book *Housekeeping Hints*: "Don't feel you have to bathe your baby every day. He won't tell anybody."[17]

 Share: Share what you chose to do on your socials with #ParentingWithSelfCompassion or at DrJenFerris.com.

In this chapter, we discussed how we can improve as parents when we let go of trying to be "perfect."

Another way to become better parents is to look at how we were raised. Are you reacting in ways similar to how your parents behaved? Is this what you want or don't want? Let's take a look.

Chapter 3

What We Carry—What to Keep and Discard

"The Golden Rule of Parenting is to do unto your children as you wish your parents had done unto you!"

Louise Hart

My parents were not perfect, but there were parts of how I grew up that I wanted to include in my own parenting. I made a choice in my twenties to keep doing the cultural, religious, and family practices that I had enjoyed growing up.

In the back of your mind, if it isn't too painful, think about your childhood. What were some of the ways your main caregivers parented you? Fingers crossed there are some positive memories.

If there were things you loved, decide to continue doing those, if you aren't already. Perhaps there are specific parenting behaviors you enjoyed, such as a tickle monster or going out for ice cream after a game or show. Your mom or dad, your grandparents, or whoever you lived with as a child, were your role models; hopefully they did some things that you want to keep doing in your life.

Next, I want you to think about the practices you were raised with that you didn't like, maybe because they felt unfair. If you didn't like how it felt to be spanked, yelled at, or sent to your room, you can decide to change the script. There are many ways to parent. New techniques can be learned.

Choosing to parent differently can be beneficial; it can help make each generation better than the last. Making this choice doesn't mean you're saying that you had bad parents. Most parents love their children deeply and try to do their best. Our parents were likely trying to do better than their own. Perhaps they succeeded.

If we can think of our parents as people and see that they struggled, then we can have compassion for them. This allows us to separate ourselves from them, and parent our own children to the best of our ability.

You Don't Have to Become Like Your Parents

My younger child asked me one day, "Why do I have to?"

I replied quickly with, "Because I said so!"

And as soon as the words left my lips, I thought, "Oh no, I sound just like my mother!"

Has that ever happened to you? I hated being told, "Because I said so" as a kid, but like George Santayana[1] famously said, "Those who cannot remember the past are condemned to repeat it."

If we push things down and avoid thinking about how we were parented, we can later become those parents, saying and doing the exact same things that we didn't like as children.

When people are under stress, they tend
to do what they know.

That's why the things that happened to us as children can have a big impact on us as adults.

Becoming parents often brings up issues from childhood.

17

But we can notice when this happens and change our behaviors, to become more in sync with how we want to be as parents.[2]

It can help to think about when we get triggered by our kids' actions or words. When we see that happening, we can change the pattern and replace it with something new. Being conscious and aware is the first step toward change.

There was a time in my childhood when I was weighed daily. It made me feel awful about myself, so I chose not to do that with my children. Instead, I tell them to "listen to your body" to know when they are hungry, when they are full, and what they want to eat. Ultimately, they will be living on their own and in charge of their own food choices.

Childhood Trauma

It's estimated that 60 percent of American adults[3] and 70 percent of adults worldwide[4] have experienced at least one traumatic event in their lives.

Childhood trauma occurs when kids are exposed to upsetting and painful situations, such as sexual or physical abuse, neglect, death, kidnapping, car accidents, natural disasters, or witnessing violence and abuse.

If this includes you, it's important to get treatment from a qualified mental health professional who's trained in trauma therapy. This work is emotionally difficult, but remember, you're doing it for yourself and for your kids.

Therapy can help you notice unhealthy patterns and learn coping tools to improve your mental health, relationships, and parenting. For more assistance check out Trauma Free World, The National Child Traumatic Stress Network, Child Trauma Academy, and Trauma-Focused Cognitive-Behavioral Therapy.

Sit and Think: How was I parented? How did that make me feel? What, if anything, do I want to do the same? What, if anything, do I want to do differently?

 Action: As things come up, and as your kids get older, you can start to tell them how you were raised and why you are choosing to do things the same or differently with them.

 Share: Share what you have decided to do the same or differently from your own childhood on your socials with #ParentingWithSelfCompassion or at DrJenFerris.com.

No matter what traditions and behaviors we decide to keep or get rid of from how we were raised, as parents we will likely need a great deal of support from those around us.

Chapter 4

You Don't Have to Do It All on Your Own

"I believe the world is one big family, and we need to help each other."

Jet Li

With my first baby, when I was exhausted and "in it," I was just trying to survive.

I didn't ask for help because I didn't realize asking for help was even an option.

Once it was pointed out to me—and it had to be—I was finally able to accept help. It seemed that if I asked for help, then I wasn't a good mom. As a first-time parent, I felt isolated and like I had to do it all on my own.

Asking for Help is the Right Thing to Do!

Some new parents live with family or friends, while others live too far away or may not have family in their lives. Whatever the situation may be, it's easier to survive those early months with the support of people who care about you and your kids. Friends, family, volunteers, and hired professionals may have different experiences and perspectives to share that make you think about or try things in a new way.

Unsolicited advice can be annoying and you certainly don't have to take every suggestion on board, but some new ideas may be beneficial. I didn't have family living nearby, but I was lucky enough to have family and friends I knew cared.

Late one night, I called my dad, crying. "This is really hard! Is it ever going to get better?" He didn't sugarcoat it when he said, "It will get easier, but it will take time, and then it will feel like two steps forward, one step back."

I was disappointed that nothing was fixed, but it was nice to know that I wasn't the only one who had ever gone through this.

Why had it been so hard for me to make that call? During my pregnancy, many people told me I could contact them anytime. Why didn't I reach out when I was in need, and why don't so many new parents take up friends and family on this offer?

We might be embarrassed, too exhausted to think straight, or we may believe deep down that we should be able to do it on our own.

In the US, where I live, there is a huge focus on independence and making your own way. We can feel pressure to look like we have it all together.

The message we get from society is, "You shouldn't need help." But in reality, it's normal to not know what to do sometimes. And it's not only okay, but it's good for you and your kids, if you ask other people for help. Requesting assistance is not a sign of weakness and it doesn't mean you're a bad parent; it means you're human.

Find ways to allow yourself to be supported by friends, family, and your community. Research shows that people who feel more connected to others have less depression and anxiety, higher self-esteem, and greater well-being.[1] That sounds pretty good to me.

How to Ask for Help

It can be hard to ask for help. You might feel like you're imposing on and bothering them, feel afraid they'll say no, or feel ashamed that something is wrong with you. But these thoughts are not true. We all need support sometimes, especially when we're raising children. And who doesn't love to hold a baby?

If someone offers to bring by food, help with cleaning, or spend time with the baby, try not to say, "Oh, no no no, we're fine." Instead, accept their offer with gratitude, because in addition to benefiting your life and the life of your family, it can also make them feel good and useful too.

When you ask for help, be specific about what you need, so that you can get what will bring you the most relief. Do you want someone to come over and do the dishes, bring food and coffee, or vacuum up the dog hair that's taking over your living room?

It can be useful to have a to-do list out ready to go, so that if someone is visiting and asks how they can help, you can just hand them the list and say, "Pick an item. Thanks so much!"[2]

Asking for help when needed is important for you and your family. Parents who feel supported have more self-confidence, better mental health, and more positive relationships with their kids.[3]

This may be a new skill, but it's one that, with practice, we can all learn. It's also a great gift to show your children that you know your limits, and you can accept help when you need it.

Tips for Before and After a New Baby

Think and talk about what your needs will be once the baby is born

Who will be in the home with you? Who can give you a break?

The idea is to set up a support system before the baby comes, while still leaving room to be flexible, in case you need different things once the baby arrives.[4] Do you have a family member you trust who will help take care of you and the baby? Are you able to get a postpartum doula (we'll get to that soon) and a lactation consultant, if needed?

Do the things that only you can do

When I felt overwhelmed taking care of a newborn, my husband's advice to me was to "do the things only you can do." When I felt like I needed to do the dishes or laundry, I asked myself, "Can someone else do this?" If the answer was yes, then I tried really hard not to do it. I fed or rested with the baby—things that only I could do.

Everything else (dishes, laundry, trash, grocery store run, watering the plants, walking the dog) I wrote down on a list in the kitchen for my partner to start working on when he got home. Sometimes, the most important thing was for him to take the baby so I could have a break or a shower. I was lucky to have this help. For single parents is there a friend, family member, or paid caregiver who can come over to give you a break?

Have a 15-minute check-in

If there's more than one adult in the home, take 15 minutes each day to talk about what happened during the day (or night!), the positive moments, and the challenges. See if there's anything the other person can do to help with the struggles.

There was a point after having my first child when I was pretty dehydrated, like dizzy and fainting, but I was so sleep deprived I couldn't think of a way to solve the problem. I talked to my husband about it one night, and he thought of putting a fresh water bottle next to each chair where I fed the baby. The visual cue reminded me to drink water every time I fed her. It totally worked!

Place an ad at a local college for a babysitter

If, at any point, you want to hire a babysitter, in addition to checking out online sites, think about placing an ad at a local college with a preference for the major that is going to be a teacher (liberal studies, child development, early childhood education, or whatever the subject is where you live). An ad can usually be placed online with the college's career center. To interview possible sitters, you can have them come to your home if your child is young, or you can meet them at a nearby coffee shop.

Ask questions about their experience working with children, classes they've taken about children, what they want to do after college, how much they expect to make, their availability, and how many hours they want to work per week. Are they a full- or part-time student? Do they have another job? Get to know them and see if they're a good fit.

You may want to do a Google search of them to make sure there aren't a thousand pictures of them partying and talking about how they blew off work. Yes, of course that's happened to me.

Most importantly, go with your gut;
trust your instincts as a parent.

Help After a New Baby

In the United States, after a birth, there are check-ups for the baby, but no one checks in on how the mothers or fathers are doing. Compare this to the Netherlands, where a home maternity nurse goes into the home to help for three to eight hours a day, for at least ten days after the birth.[5]

This in-home nurse teaches the new parent(s) about breastfeeding, changing diapers, and how to give a newborn a bath—life skills that all new parents need to know but were probably not taught in school. Home maternity nurses can also help with grocery shopping, laundry, taking care of the other children in the house, and referrals for outside services.[6]

We can't all move to the Netherlands. So wouldn't it be nice if we could have a home maternity nurse, no matter where we lived? Let's look at what life is like in the US right now after having a baby.

Parental Leave

My husband took one week of *unpaid* leave (so basically sick days) when our first baby was born. When he left after that week to go back to work, I cried hysterically and begged him not to leave me alone with the baby.

Can you relate to this feeling?

The United States is one of only six countries in the world that, at the time of writing, doesn't support their citizens with job-protected, paid time off work when they have a baby.[7]

So why does paid leave even matter?

Companies[8] who offer paid leave have

- more engaged employees
- higher productivity
- better retention.

New moms[9] with paid leave have

- lower stress
- better birth outcomes
- healthier blood pressure
- less risk of rehospitalization
- less depression.

New dads[10] with paid leave

- bond with their infant and are more involved and nurturing throughout the child's life
- do more housework over time
- develop more empathy
- promote gender equality
- support their partner's financial independence.

The babies[11] of parent(s) with paid leave have

- lower infant mortality rates
- more sensitive interactions with parents because of less parental stress
- better immunity because of more breastfeeding
- mature early cognitive functioning
- good language skills as toddlers
- less behavior problems.

People in the happiest countries in the world like Finland benefit from the best parental leave policies.[12] This is not a coincidence. Parental leave affects the entire family.

When new parents are given paid time off after a birth, it reduces financial stress and allows for time to bond with the child. It's society's way of telling new parents that being an at-home parent is a valued and respected, full-time job.

Paid parental leave acknowledges the time that's needed to physically and emotionally recover after having a new baby. Plus, the older kids in the home get to see all of this being modeled.[13]

But if you live in a country like the US that currently doesn't have a generous parental leave policy, what can you do? Besides family and friends, what support is out there for new parents like you?

Support for New Parents

According to OB-GYN Dr. Angelica Glover,[14] having a postpartum support network is important after having a new baby. If you're stuck at home after the baby arrives and you want to talk to others in the same situation, there is Postpartum Support International (PSI).

Postpartum doula

If you don't have help and you can afford it, you can hire a postpartum doula—a person who helps take care of the newborn, offers emotional support, and provides information on feeding, soothing, and newborn care.[15]

Postpartum doulas can assist with light housekeeping, running errands, taking care of siblings, light meal preparation, making doctor appointments, and giving referrals.

Where I'm based, the cost varies between $15 and $50 an hour, depending on experience, location, and the services provided. Postpartum doulas have become popular recently, with parents-to-be asking for them as a baby shower gift.[16]

To find one you can ask your doctor or midwife for referrals, google "postpartum doula" and where you live, or go to International Childbirth Education Association, DONA (Doula of North America) International, DoulaMatch, or CAPPA (Childbirth and Postpartum Professional Association).

When you talk with a postpartum doula, find out their qualifications, how many families they've worked with, the cost, and what services they provide.[17] Just like with your doctor, midwife, and doula during the pregnancy, you want to feel comfortable with this person after the birth.

La Leche League

La Leche League (LLL) offers free meetings in over 80 countries, including the United States and the United Kingdom.[18] At LLL meetings, new parents talk about breastfeeding challenges and get ideas on ways to make feeding easier.

A downside is that if the meeting is too far away it can be difficult for new parents to attend. Going to LLL meetings when my baby was young gave me the confidence to reach out to a lactation consultant later on.

Lactation consultants

A lactation consultant is a trained and certified healthcare professional who helps people with breastfeeding and bodyfeeding, pumping, and feeding issues, using education and hands-on learning. When a parent realizes they need one, time is often of the essence. That's why it's good to already have a professional lined up, just in case.[19]

Breastfeeding and chestfeeding are natural processes, but many people encounter problems and need help. You can get referrals from doulas, midwives, and doctors, as well as from family and friends who live in your area.

To find a qualified lactation consultant you can search directories, such as the United States Lactation Consultant Association (USLCA) in the US and Lactation Consultants of Great Britain (LCGB) in the UK. In the US, there is a breastfeeding helpline at 1-800-994-9662. Boober can also match you with a lactation consultant as well as other professionals and classes in your area.

In addition to support from professionals, non-professional support is crucial when you become a parent.

Meeting Other Parents

Find ways to meet and get together with other parents to talk about the stress, fears, fatigue, joys, tears, and the general highs and lows of parenthood. Parenting can be lonely, and it helps to know you aren't the only one feeling this way.

Other parents can offer understanding, laughter, suggestions, local recommendations, and a feeling of community and togetherness.

In person, you can meet other parents at

- the library and bookstore storytimes
- the park
- coffee shops
- breastfeeding and bodyfeeding support groups
- parent and baby yoga
- new parent support groups
- community centers and religious organizations
- Gymboree Play & Music or other music classes
- local parent groups on Facebook or Meetup.

MOMS Club

Going to a local MOMS Club meeting can be a good way to share your feelings and get and give advice and support.[20]

A few months after my first child was born, I found a local MOMS Club, and it was a lifesaver. My first outing was a get-together at the leader's house. It was so nice to get out of my home for a few hours, play with new toys, have some snacks, and talk to other adults.

Then we broke off into smaller groups based on our kids' ages. Everyone who had a child born in the same year met up at a local park. When we felt comfortable, the four of us and our children started doing a weekly playgroup at each other's houses or at a park, depending on the weather.

It was great for the kids to play together and for the parents to talk about our struggles and get support. If one of us had an emergency or a new birth, we could call on each other.

If you're interested, do a Google search for MOMS Club and your area. If there isn't one, think about starting a new chapter. This would be a huge help to you and to the other parents in your neighborhood.

Social media, the internet, and other sources

To find other parents on Facebook, Meetup, and Google, you can search for "mom's group," "dad's group," or "parenting group" and your location. If you're parenting multiples, raising a child on your own, or have a preemie, there may be specific groups for you. It can feel awkward at first, but you'd be surprised how many parents are open to talking.

You can also check out Peanut, an international app to meet other parents nearby who are at the same stage as you. I have even met people when exchanging free or low-cost maternity and children's clothes using apps like Craigslist.

Activities for a fee include Gymboree Play & Music classes, YMCA Kids Club, Music Together, and Local Mommy and Me or Parent and Me classes.

Therapy

Therapy can help us learn what to do when our buttons get pushed. It can enable us to strengthen our mental health, become more self-aware, and create better relationships.

People can find new ways to cope with and manage their stress. Some people decide to work through challenging life events or traumas. Therapy is an important part of treating mental health conditions, such as postpartum depression, anxiety, PTSD, and eating disorders.

Going to therapy can be difficult at first, but it can result in a more satisfying life and a closer relationship with your child.

One way to find a therapist is to go to PsychologyToday.com and click on "Find A Therapist." Once you put in your city or postal code, you can filter by the type of therapy, your insurance provider, the gender of the therapist, and the issue you want the therapist to be good at treating, such as anxiety, depression, addiction, grief, relationship, or anger issues.

If you tap on the pictures of the therapists, they describe themselves, and you can get a sense of their personality. They may also have a link to their website and ways to contact them for a free call, to see if you're a good fit.

If you try to find a therapist through your insurance provider, often not much information is given. You can filter by gender, age, location, and who is taking new patients. You can also google them to get more information.

If you're in high school, there's often a free school counselor, and if you're in college, you can go to the health center or the psychology department for treatment and referrals.

You want to be sure to find a therapist you match well with, one who will be supportive yet challenging, so progress can be made.

During the free consultation, you can ask if they're licensed in your state and if they have experience working with people who are dealing with your issue(s). What do they specialize in? What treatment methods do they use? Can they prescribe medication? If not, you may need to see a separate psychiatrist.

Does the therapist take your insurance, and if not, what would the fee be? Many therapists offer therapy via Zoom.[21]

Some people have found therapists and gotten more information using these resources:

- American Psychological Association (APA)
- Therapy Den
- Mental Health Match
- Neurodivergent Therapists
- Momwell Maternal Mental Health Specialists

Additional resources:

- Teen Counseling
- Association of LGBTQ+ Psychiatrists (AGLP)
- Therapy for Black Girls
- Black Mental Health Alliance
- Therapy for Latinx
- The National Asian American Pacific Islander Mental Health Association (NAAPIMHA)
- Yellow Chair Collective (YCC)
- WeRNative
- Anxiety and Depression Association of America (ADAA)
- National Center for PTSD
- National Eating Disorders Association (NEDA)
- American Association of Marriage and Family Therapists (AAMFT)

Sit and Think: What do I need help with? How can I get the support I need?

 Action: When you've found an area of your life in which you could use help, take one small step toward getting support.

 Share: In what areas of your life could you use some help? What small actions are you taking to get the assistance that you need and deserve? Please share your thoughts and actions on your socials with #ParentingWithSelfCompassion or at DrJenFerris.com.

Most people need support from family and friends throughout parenthood. As you work to be the best parent you can be, remember that you don't have to do it alone. Be willing to ask for help—in doing so, you show your child how to do the same.

Just as those around us affect our experience of being a parent, the words we use with our kids affect them too.

But why do the words we use even matter?

Chapter 5

"Walk, Please." Why Wording Matters

"Good words are worth much, and cost little."

George Herbert

Okay, right now, *don't* think of a giraffe!
What are you picturing? A giraffe, right? Of course you are, because that's how the human brain works. When you hear a word, you think of it.

When parents yell, "Don't run!", children hear, "Run!" and they want to keep running.
Instead, try:

> Please use your walking feet.

Or:

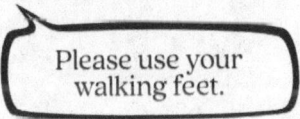

> Walk inside, please.

33

I know it doesn't roll off the tongue, but when children hear "walk," it tells them exactly what you want them to do.

Tell Children What You Want Them to Do

When we tell our children to stop doing something, their brains may not be developed enough to understand what that means.[1] Adults can think of the opposite of something pretty well, such as hot and cold or up and down. But little kids may still be learning this concept—that's why there are so many books and games about opposites.

There can also be confusion about what behavior to stop, if parents use vague words like "Stop that!", "Quit it!", or "Don't do that!" The child might think, "I'm doing a lot of things right now, like eating, humming, and twirling my hair. Which one am I supposed to stop doing?"[2]

Another downside to saying, "Don't kick your brother!" is that we aren't telling the child what we want them to do.[3]

You scream at your kids, "Don't hit!"
Instead, try:

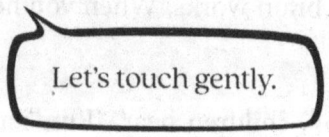

Let's touch gently.

Your child is jumping on you. You yell, "Quit it!"
Instead, try:

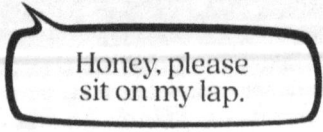

Honey, please
sit on my lap.

Your kids are being too loud in the house. You scream, "Shut up!"
Instead try:

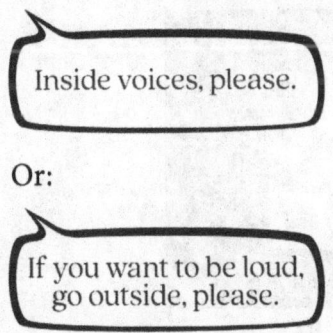

Inside voices, please.

Or:

If you want to be loud,
go outside, please.

When I first moved to town, I saw a huge sign on the side of the road that read: "Don't text and drive!"

What did that sign make me want to do? Yes, you got it, it made me want to text, which I hadn't even been thinking about doing! That was not what the good people who made the sign had wanted my reaction to be.

A few months later, the sign was gone, replaced by a new sign that read: "Please slow down." This was better because it told me what they wanted me to do; namely, to slow down. Then I was saying in my head, "Slow down" instead of "Text and drive."

But could there be an even better way to get the desired message across? A month later, in the same area, I saw a sign that read: "Drive 25!"

It says what it wants me to do—drive 25 miles per hour—and it rhymes! I will never forget this phrase now, and I notice that I tend to go slower on that street.

Does it take a little more time and effort to think of a positive way to say something (I'm looking at you, freeway signs in California)? Yes, but it's worth it.

Tips with Words

More statements, fewer questions

Sometimes parents ask a question and their child responds with, "No!" Instead, you can give a request or a statement.

Let's say you usually ask something like, "Do you want to help me clean this up?"

Instead try:

> The drink is spilled. Grab a towel and help me wipe it up please.

Or you might make a request like "Can you share that with your brother, please?"

Instead try:

> Please share that with your brother. You also like it when he shares with you.

These statements are more likely to be followed than questions.

Try not to label your kids

For better or worse, our children believe what we say and our words help shape who they become.[4]

In fact, labels can become self-fulfilling prophecies.[5]

As a kid, when I was introduced to new adults, I tended to grab my parent's hand or leg. I often heard, "Oh, she's shy." I remember thinking, "I guess I'm shy."

Also, if your kids say they can't do something, remind them that they can't do it yet.

When the time feels right, you could say to your child:

> *"When something is important to you, if you keep practicing, almost anything is possible."*

Talk about the behavior, not the child

A parent says, "You're a bad boy."
Instead, try:

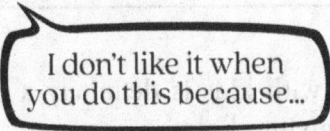

I don't like it when you do this because...

When you call someone a "bad boy" or a "bad girl," you're saying they're a bad person at their core, and that is a hard thing to overcome. But if there's a specific thing you don't like them doing, that is much easier to change. You didn't like what your kid did, but they aren't a bad person.

Your first instinct is to say, "You're such a slob!"
Instead, try:

> When you go out in your pajamas, I worry that people may get the wrong impression of you.

 Sit and Think: What are some things you say to your child? How might these statements make them feel? How would you feel if someone said that to you?

 Action: Try saying something in a new way. How does it go over with your child? How do you feel after saying it in this different way?

 Share: Share what you used to say and what you say now on your socials with #ParentingWithSelfCompassion or at DrJenFerris.com.

While choosing kind words with kids is definitely a plus, another useful strategy is that of giving choices.

Chapter 6

This or That?
Offering Choices

*"Listen to the desires of your children. Encourage them and
then give them the autonomy to make their own decision."*
Denis Waitley

When I was making dinner for my 6-year-old, I asked her,
"Do you want carrots or peas with your dinner?" That
night, she went with the peas.

I wanted her to have a vegetable with dinner, but if I'd just
picked one and put it on her plate, she might not have eaten it.
There would've been no buy in.

But when she makes the choice about which vegetable to
put on her plate, she's happier and more likely to eat it, and I'm
pleased that she's eating something healthy. So, it's a win-win.

Give Kids Choices, but Not Too Many

When children are offered choices, they learn to make
decisions and solve problems, gain confidence, and feel like they
have some control over their lives.[1]

Say, for example, you give your son a choice between two outfits. When he picks one and gets a compliment from his teacher, he feels pride in his selection.

If your daughter chooses to wear her favorite shoes to school on a rainy day and they get muddy, she learns which shoes she'd rather not wear on a rainy day.

You pose to your toddler:

> Do you want to walk to the changing table or should I carry you?

When she lifts her arms up and says, "Up-y," the choice has been made.

You ask your preschooler:

> Hey Sweetie, do you want to wear the red shirt or the blue top today?

Offering choices gives your child the opportunity to be part of the decision-making process and it increases the likelihood of cooperation. No one likes to be given orders, and children are no different.

You can make the choices fun:[2]

> It's time to go. Do you want to run or skip to the car?

Offering your child a choice can help with bonding and better communication.

Presenting a kid with choices builds trust and respect with the adult because the child feels valued.[3]

It improves your relationship with your child because they'll feel empowered and want to cooperate with you.[4]

It's also more respectful to give choices than to tell a child what they have to do.[5]

Tantrums can happen when children feel like they don't have any power. Giving kids choices can reduce conflicts and lead to fewer tantrums, because children feel like they have a say in the things that affect them.[6]

Even when it's not practical or possible to offer choices, acknowledging that your child has an input in things can go far:

I can't give you a choice for veggies tonight because we only have carrots. When I go to the store tomorrow there will be more options.

Tips on Giving Choices

Give children two choices

One choice isn't a choice—it's a command. Three or more choices can feel overwhelming. When there are too many choices, kids can have trouble deciding, may regret their final choice, and they spend less time engaged with their choice, like playing less with the toy they chose.

Instead, narrow down the choices to two:

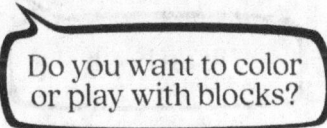

Do you want to color or play with blocks?

Don't put "okay" at the end of your sentence to try to soften it

I used to do this all the time when I worked in childcare. When you say:

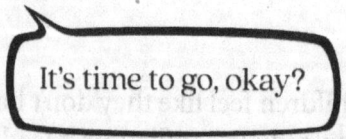

It's time to go, okay?

It makes it sound like a question, and the child will say, "No!" Instead, after giving a warning, you can state:

It's time for us to go.

Or:

Say 'bye bye' and I'll race you to the door.

Don't offer a choice if there isn't one

If kids have to do something, don't make it seem like they have a choice. A parent asks:

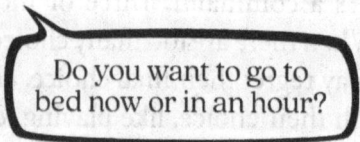

Do you want to go to bed now or in an hour?

The child responds:

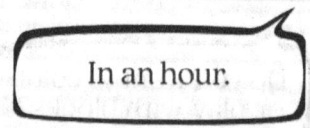

In an hour.

The parent replies:

> No, you have to
> go to bed now!

The kid wonders:

> Then why did you
> give me the choice?

The parent concludes:

> Because I was tired, and
> I wasn't thinking straight.

Don't say that last part.

Only offer choices you're okay with

You don't want to be hoping your child picks one option over the other—you've got to be okay with either choice.

If you're not cool with your child drinking chocolate milk, then don't ask, "Do you want water, milk, or chocolate milk?"

Your child will, for sure, choose the chocolate milk, so only give choices you can agree to and save yourself the struggle later on.

Don't assume that giving choices will always work

Your child might not like the two choices you offer and say, "none," or suggest their own choice that you're not okay with.[7]

You can ask your child for suggestions, and try to work with them to find a compromise you can both be happy with.

Let's say you wonder:

> Do you want an
> apple or crackers?

Your child says:

> I want cookies.

You reply:

> I hear you want cookies, but
> we don't have them. What snack
> would you like that we have
> in the kitchen?

 Sit and Think: What are some choices I can
offer my child? Can I picture how my child might
respond when given these options?

 Action: Try giving your child two choices. How
does your child respond? How did it feel?

 Share: Share what you used to say and
what you say now on your socials with
#ParentingWithSelfCompassion or at
DrJenFerris.com.

While offering children choices is a good tool to use, another
parenting tip is to pick and choose your battles.

Chapter 7

Not Every Fight
Is Worth Fighting

"Choose your battles wisely. After all, life is too short to spend it on warring. Fight only the most, most, most important ones, let the rest go."

C. Joybell C.

When I walk by my younger kid's bedroom and see that she's left the light on, I mostly just turn it off for her. I ask her to turn off the light when she leaves her room because it's wasteful and it bothers me an abnormal amount. I was brought up in a home where you turned off the lights when you left a room. But right now, it isn't that big a deal.

Children are well aware that they lack power and the adult is in charge. You know how I know? Children can't have ice cream or candy whenever they want. Nor can they go to their friend's house unless you say it's okay.

As parents, we don't need to prove that we're in charge. We also don't have to fight with our kids over every little thing.

Tips about Conflicts

Pick and choose your battles

As parents when we pick and choose our battles:

We are making a choice to not fight over the small things.

If we bother our kids about every little thing, it will become too much and they may stop listening to us and talking with us.

This can be a problem when we need to talk with them later on about the bigger things, like driving, drugs, and sex. Having a good relationship with your child is important in the long run.

How do we decide which issues need to be discussed and which ones we can let go of? One thing I think about when deciding is, "Could this hurt my child or someone else?"

If safety is a concern, you can't let it go. If a child is running out into the street after a ball and there's a car coming, you have to grab them fast, then talk to them about it afterward. In the same way, if a child is hitting, kicking, or verbally harming another child, an adult needs to intervene.

Let the small stuff go

There are many things that parents can just let be and move on from. In a video I used to show in class, there was a single mother putting her daughter to bed. The child wanted to wear a hat to bed and the mother yelled, "No!", grabbed the hat, and spanked her. The experts asked the mother, "What's the worst thing that can happen? She wears the hat to bed; she gets hot, she takes it off."

The mother thought that if it was the hat today, then it would be something else tomorrow. "Let's deal with that then," they said.

Talk with children about things that affect their health, relationships, and school experience:

- If they don't brush their teeth, they'll get cavities and it won't be a fun day at the dentist.

- If they stay up too late on a school night, they will likely be tired and have a harder time at school the next day.
- When their backpack is extremely disorganized, it may be hard to find homework to turn in to the teacher.

Let go of the small things that don't actually cause big problems

Small things to let go of include how your child ties their shoes, what they choose to wear, how well they brush their hair, where they do their homework, and that their grades could be a little higher.[1]

If they want to do their homework in bed or standing up, who cares as long as it's getting done? Choosing the important things to discuss with your kids, and not harping on about every little thing, will lead to a happier environment and a stronger bond.

 Sit and Think: What's a small thing that I can let go of with my child? What's the worst that could happen?

 Action: Let one or two small things go. What happened? Was it the end of the world, or was it okay?

 Share: Share what you chose to let go of and how it went on your socials with #ParentingWithSelfCompassion or at DrJenFerris.com.

Picking and choosing your battles is important in having a harmonious home. It can also help to look at things from your child's perspective.

Chapter 8

Walk in Their Shoes— a Lesson in Gaining Perspective

"The greatest tragedy for any human being is going through their entire life believing the only perspective that matters is their own."

Doug Baldwin

L ook at the picture. What do you see?

MY WIFE AND MY MOTHER-IN-LAW
They are both in this picture — Find them

When I first started teaching, I saw a young lady with a hat. Now, I see an older woman turned to the side.

This famous picture is called *My Wife and My Mother-in-Law* and is also known as *Boring Figure*. It was drawn by cartoonist W.E. Hill in 1915.

A 2018 study found that people between 18 and 30 tend to see the young woman first, and people over 30 are more likely to view the older woman first.[1]

Two people can look at the same image and see different things. Our age affects us unconsciously in the way we view things.

Kids are Egocentric

Children are egocentric; they can't see things from another person's point of view. They believe that others see, hear, feel, and think the same way they do.[2]

It's not that they're selfish—they just can't understand different perspectives yet. This is a skill that develops over time. As children get older and their brains develop more, they can see other people's points of view more easily.[3]

Examples of egocentrism

When I used to play hide-and-seek with my young daughter, she'd sit on the couch and put her hands over her eyes. She thought if she couldn't see me, then I couldn't see her. Well, I could see her, so she didn't do very well at hide-and-seek. Until later on, when she discovered that her small size was a strength and she hid in the hamper!

A young boy is crying. A little girl can tell he's upset so she gives him her favorite stuffed animal because it always makes her feel better. She thinks that what comforts her will comfort him too.[4]

A girl grabs a toy from another child. She isn't thinking about how her actions make that child feel. She just wants the toy, so she takes it.

Look at Things From the Child's Point of View

If there are young children in a room, crawl around on the floor and see things from their perspective. What does the room look like? Is it safe or are there sharp items on the carpet, or toys that could fall down on them? Are the pictures where the kids can see them or are they at the adult's eye level?

As parents we tend to see things from our own point of view, but the child's point of view matters too. Just like we want our children to be able to take their friend's perspective, we can try to see things from our kid's point of view, to be more curious about how they see things and why. When we know how they're thinking, we can improve our interactions with them and how we respond to them.

The golden rule says we should treat others how we would want to be treated, but, shouldn't we treat others how *they* would want to be treated? Isn't that even better?

People may think and want different things from us.

Encourage your kids to imagine how others are thinking and feeling. This is one of the first steps to your children becoming caring people.

Ask questions like: "How do you think you would feel if your friend did that to you?"

We can model perspective-taking. Next time someone cuts you off in traffic, now I know this is tough, but you can say:

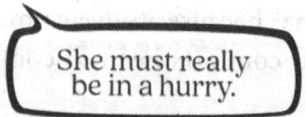

She must really be in a hurry.

Or when someone is rude to you at a store, you can say:

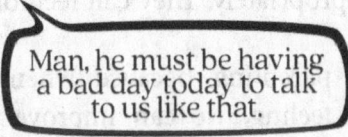

Man, he must be having a bad day today to talk to us like that.

Explain to your children that you're not perfect. Maybe you have a lot on your plate right now and you didn't respond in the best way. Admit that you messed up and you're working on improving. This helps them see things from your perspective.

It Begins with Empathy

Empathy is understanding how someone else is feeling and responding appropriately. It's imagining what it would be like to walk in the other person's shoes.[5]

 Did you know? When you have empathy for someone, you produce fewer stress hormones and more positive hormones that help reduce pain, boost immunity, and improve your health.[6]

People with empathy

- are happier and more often satisfied with their lives
- have less stress, anxiety, and depression
- are more likely to have happy, successful relationships
- are more successful at work
- make better leaders because they can see their employee's perspective
- are kinder and more generous
- feel more connected to others
- have higher self-esteem
- communicate well and have fewer conflicts.[7]

People with empathy can read coworkers' feelings and nonverbal cues, and respond appropriately. They can feel for an employee who has a sick child.

Empathy is important in parenting because when we understand how our kids are feeling, we can improve our interactions with them, respond with less anger, and be better able to prevent meltdowns—all because we understand where our kids are coming from.[8]

When we're empathetic with our children, they feel validated and heard. And then, because of that feeling they tend to be more willing to cooperate. It aids our relationships with our kids and shows them how to be empathetic toward others.[9]

Empathy can be taught. It can grow by trying to imagine how others are feeling when you're talking with them, practicing reading their body language, putting down electronics and paying closer attention, and asking questions.[10]

When children spend time with babies it can build empathy. Roots of Empathy is a school program that started in Canada, in which a local parent brings their baby into the classroom throughout the year.

The students can ask questions, watch the baby play, talk about how the baby might be feeling, and see things from the infant's point of view.

The kids learn empathy as it gets their thinking off themselves and their own wants, and onto those of another person.

On YouTube, you can search for Roots of Empathy or go to DrJenFerris.com for more information.

Tips for Teaching Empathy

Model it

If they're able to, children tend to behave the way they see their parents act. When our kids see us bring soup to a sick friend or offer a neighbor a ride, they become more likely to show empathy and kindness too.

Ask questions, listen to their answers, and be curious

Empathy grows from face-to-face interactions.

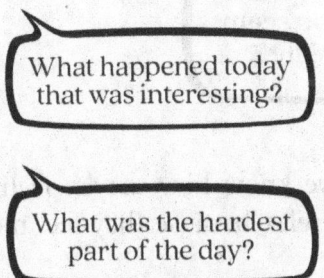

We're showing that we're interested in their lives and not just our own. We can be vulnerable, open up, and explain that we've felt that way before too.

When there are conflicts, have family meetings where everyone can talk and family members can see each other's points of view.

At dinner, ask them about their friends, their favorite foods, books, and movies. Talk about issues that came up at school. What is a good way to behave? We're raising our children to become upstanders, who will stand up for others because they know it's the right thing to do.

Name how you feel, help your kids say how they're feeling, and ask others how they might feel

I might say:

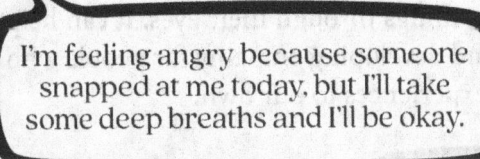

When we talk about our emotions, it helps our kids understand the feelings and thoughts of others, and how to label and express their own feelings too.

We might say to our child:

> You're clenching your fists and stomping on the ground. You seem angry right now. Is that right?

When our children can tell we know how they're feeling, it can help them calm down and relax because they feel more understood.

Express yourself when your child shows empathy without being asked

If we value kindness the same way we value academics, then just as we compliment our kids when they do well at school, we can also let them know we're proud of them when they show empathy.

> Thank you for getting an ice pack so your sister would feel better. That was kind and helpful of you.

Read books and watch movies with characters from different backgrounds

Reading books with characters from other cultures can allow us to better see things through their eyes. It can help with perspective taking and developing empathy for people who have lived with different experiences to our own.

> How do you think he feels?

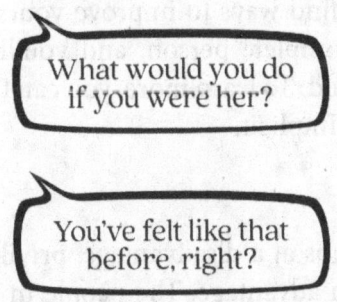

Interact with people from other backgrounds

Volunteer in your community. Encourage your kids to get a pen pal from another place in the world.

Talking with others can decrease our prejudices and biases, making it easier to have empathy. When we see the things that we have in common with people, there's less fear and more understanding.

Cooperative board games and meditations, such as the loving kindness meditation, can also help build empathy toward other people. See the Bonus section on meditation for more information.

Admit that you're likely biased

We are all most likely biased, but often our biases are unconscious, so we may not know we have them. Common biases have to do with gender, race, class, sexual orientation, age, weight, and culture.

Having these biases affects our ability to have empathy for people. While it may be uncomfortable and even shame-inducing to have our unconscious biases pointed out, if we can see what they are, we can work on improving them.

If you have young children, you may be incredibly busy and you may feel like you don't have the time or energy to work on yourself in this way. Remember to be kind to yourself about this.

Maybe you can keep this in the back of your mind, and when you have some time, you might remember that you wanted to take a quiz or read a book, and find ways to improve yourself. It will help make you a more complete person, and you'll be modeling that growth for your child. To learn more, you can take an implicit bias test from Project Implicit.

Be aware of privilege

While biases put certain groups at a disadvantage, privilege puts certain societal groups at an advantage. The people in the latter get a special status, and they don't even know they're getting a benefit that others don't get.

People who don't have to worry about police violence at traffic stops, or those who know they have enough food and a safe place to sleep, are examples of people who have privileges others don't have.

Just starting to think about privilege doesn't take too much time and energy. Please note, it's not my intention to make you feel like you have yet another item to add to your to-do list. I understand that you're juggling many balls in the air.

But when you have a little downtime, you may choose to do the quiz below or read an online article. Your knowledge of these ideas will then be passed down to your kids. But, as always, be gentle with yourself.

You can take the Moving Up "American Dream Score" quiz, to find out which factors have worked in your favor and which ones you've had to overcome to get to where you are today.

Have the hard conversations

Don't worry—this is not about sex!

Talk with your kids about the beliefs and prejudices that exist in society including racism, sexism, discrimination against certain sexual orientations, gender identities, and financial inequality.

People are treated differently based on how they look. Women haven't always been able to vote and get their own bank accounts. Our kids need to know the truths in our world so they can make the world better one day.[11]

Talk to your kids as they get older about the news and current events

How might the kids who live there feel?

Is there anything we can do to help?

Empathy Quiz

If you're interested in exploring how empathic you are, try taking the free online empathy quiz from The Greater Good Science Center at the University of California, Berkeley.[12]

 Sit and Think: When I disagree with my child, can I see things from their point of view? How do I show empathy for others? Does my child see this? What can I ask my kid more about?

 Action: Ask your child questions about their day, activities, and interests. When you read with them, ask about how the characters might be feeling.

Check in with your friends, family, and neighbors to see if you can help them in some way.

 Share: Share what you asked your child and how they responded on your socials with #ParentingWithSelfCompassion or at DrJenFerris.com.

If we can improve how much empathy we have, that can only help us in our communication with our children.

Chapter 9

Communicate Effectively

"I've learned that people will forget what you said, people will forget what you did, but people will never forget how you made them feel."

Maya Angelou

U*gh, you kids are getting on my last nerve!*
They were causing a commotion in the back seat and screaming at each other. I pulled off to the side of the road and sat there, taking in some deep breaths, saying nothing. It was silent.

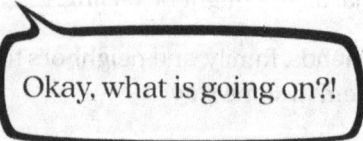

Okay, what is going on?!

Well, she was hitting me!

No, she was pinching me!

I told my younger child:

> It's not okay to touch
> her body. I need you to
> use your words when
> you're upset.

I said to the older child:

> I understand why you
> yelled, but screaming in the
> car makes it hard for
> me to drive safely.

When it seemed like we were all calm enough I said:

> Okay, if you guys are ready,
> I'm going to drive home.
> We can talk more there.

How Well We Communicate with Others Matters

Maybe, at some point, you've been seen by a medical doctor who is incredibly smart but has a horrible bedside manner. No one wants to be this doctor's patient because of the way he talks to them.

Some people may be gifted, but if they can't work well with others, it's going to be tough for them to hold down a job, maintain a relationship, and be happy and successful.

When parents communicate well with their kids, it boosts their child's self-esteem and helps to create a more positive parent–child relationship.[1]

Communication skills, when a child is able to develop them, make it easier to build friendships, do well in college, succeed in their career, and have better mental health.[2]

In 2024, having good communication skills was ranked the number one most important skill for a job applicant to have.[3] A big part of being able to communicate well with your kids is being able to listen well.

Communication Is a Two-Way Street

All too often during a conversation, when the other person is talking, we're just waiting for our chance to speak (I'm definitely guilty of this). We may be thinking about what we want to say next, or looking for a break to pipe in with our important point. When this happens, we're not doing our best at listening.

Active Listening

During active listening, parents pay close attention to what their child is saying without judging, interrupting, or giving advice.[4]

Tips for Active Listening

Look at your child and make eye contact

This helps to show that you're involved in the conversation. Some cultures may consider direct eye contact to be rude or aggressive, so make sure to know the cultural norms and when it applies, model them for your children.

Paraphrase or repeat back what your child said

...making sure you understood correctly. Some examples:

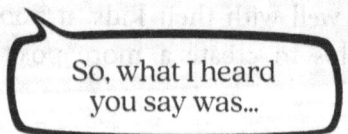

So, what I heard you say was...

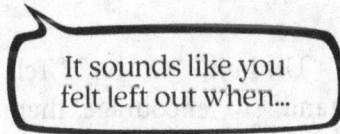

It sounds like you felt left out when...

Repeating back to a person what you heard them say can make them feel both heard and understood, leading to a better connection.

Ask open-ended questions

Open-ended questions encourage more sharing and help to clarify parts you want to understand better.

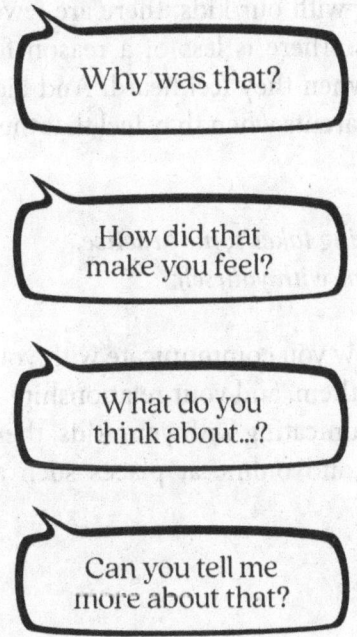

Why was that?

How did that make you feel?

What do you think about...?

Can you tell me more about that?

Use nonverbal cues to show understanding

These might include nodding, facial expressions, gestures, body language, and leaning forward. Again, this will depend on what is accepted in one's culture.

Validate your child

Say things like "I see," "Sure," "Uh huh," "Go on," "Tell me more," "Really!" and "I understand," to encourage them to continue sharing their feelings.

Remove distractions

You convey to your child that you're listening by putting away your phone, closing your laptop, and turning off the TV.

Active listening is important because it shows your children that you are paying attention and you care about what they have to say. Your children feel valued and heard, which will improve your relationship with them.

When we use active listening with our kids, there are fewer misunderstandings and conflicts. There is less of a reason for kids to get defensive or act out when they feel heard. And kids are more likely to listen to their parents when they feel that their parents are listening to them.

Being good at active listening takes some practice.
Be kind and patient with yourself.

You're working to improve how you communicate with your child and that'll be good for you, them, and your relationship.

If you'd like more help communicating with your kids, there are parenting classes in person and online at places such as FamilyCentre.org.[5]

I-Messages and U-Messages

An I-message says how you're feeling, the cause, and a possible solution:

> I get scared when you run out in the street. I worry you could get hit by a car. Please wait and walk with me next time.

Because you're just stating how *you* feel, the listener is less likely to get defensive. I-messages improve communication and empathy, and strengthen relationships.[6] They're encouraged over U-messages.

A U-message often begins with "you" and focuses on the other person's actions. "You make me so mad when you don't listen!" It accuses the other person and blames them for doing something wrong.

The listener feels attacked, gets defensive, and either denies any wrong-doing or blames you back. "You lied to me!" "No, I didn't!" It sets up a long argument.[7]

To be clear, an I-message can have the word "you" in it:

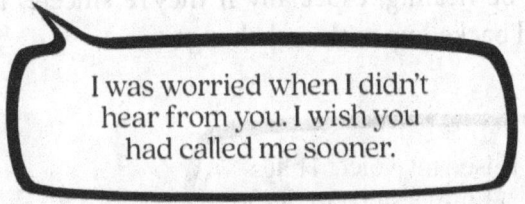

I was worried when I didn't hear from you. I wish you had called me sooner.

Here, the person is still saying how they are feeling, namely worried, explaining why, and what to do differently next time. That is vastly different from, "You should have called me sooner! What's wrong with you?"

Also, be mindful that not every sentence that starts with "I" is an I-message. "I get upset when you act so stupid!" This is clearly someone starting a sentence with an "I" when they just want to call you stupid, and that is not very nice.

Since it can be hard to remember to use I-messages when you're upset, it's suggested that parents practice using them in normal conversations to get used to doing it. It may feel strange to talk like this at first, but with practice it gets easier.

Admit When You're Wrong

It can be hard to admit to our kids when we're wrong.

If you screw up, say so. If we want our kids to acknowledge when they're wrong, we need to model that behavior. When you say you're wrong, you're telling your child that you're not perfect, but you own your mistakes, and you're working on getting better:

> You're right, I did say we would stop and get ice cream after the dentist. I forgot. We'll go do that now.

Apologies can be healing, especially if they're sincere, not used too often, and backed up with real change:

> I'm sorry I raised my voice. That's not okay. Next time I'll step out of the room and calm down before I talk to you.

Don't Force an "I'm Sorry"

Your child takes a toy from someone or hits another kid, so you insist, "Go, say you're sorry!" But what if your child isn't sorry? You're making them go over and give an insincere apology. This won't change the child's behavior or teach them empathy.

Instead, tell your child that the behavior was not okay, and then focus on the other child's feelings. This gets them thinking about the effect their behavior had on someone else.

> How do you think she's feeling?

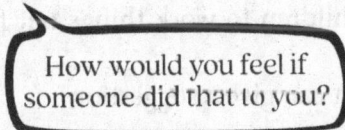

How would you feel if someone did that to you?

When we force our kids to apologize, we're telling them to be phony and pretend to feel things to please adults. An "I'm sorry" can become an excuse for bad behavior.

As parents we can model giving a real "I'm sorry" to our kids when we behave poorly, including what we plan to do differently next time. "I'm sorry I forgot to bring your stuffed animal to school. I know you missed him. I'm putting it on my calendar, so I'll remember it next time."

Try some Sportscasting

Sportscasting, coined by Magda Gerber, is when a parent narrates what's happening with a child, using a play-by-play approach. The parent describes the facts without judging, blaming, taking sides, or telling the child what to do.[8]

You seemed sad when your dad left.

You'd been trying to build that tower for a while. It was hard, but you did it.

After describing the situation, the parent can ask:

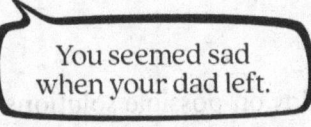

How do you think we can solve this problem?

65

The goal is for the child or children to work things out for themselves.

If the kids are stuck, the parent can give a suggestion.

> You were playing with the ball and now Destiny has it. It looks like you both want the ball. What can you do?

> Did you see that there's another ball in the basket?

The adult gets involved *if* things escalate and someone is going to get hurt. When parents use sportscasting, kids learn how to problem-solve and work out conflicts, which builds their self-confidence and shows them that we trust them to come up with solutions to problems.[9]

Problem-Solve

We can brainstorm with our kids on possible solutions to a problem. Our morning routine hadn't been working well for my child, and when I thought we were going to be late to school, I would get upset and snap.

I finally asked my pre-teen:

> Do you have any ideas that could help you get to the car on time?

She responded with:

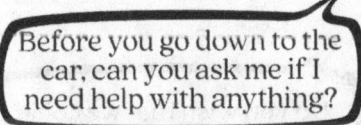

Before you go down to the car, can you ask me if I need help with anything?

It was a pretty easy request that has aided us in being on time. Sometimes I help her carry something like a posterboard down to the car, which makes it easier for her to get there, and I'm happy that we're on time.

Before your child's birthday or a gift-giving holiday, if your kid has too much stuff in their room, you might ask:

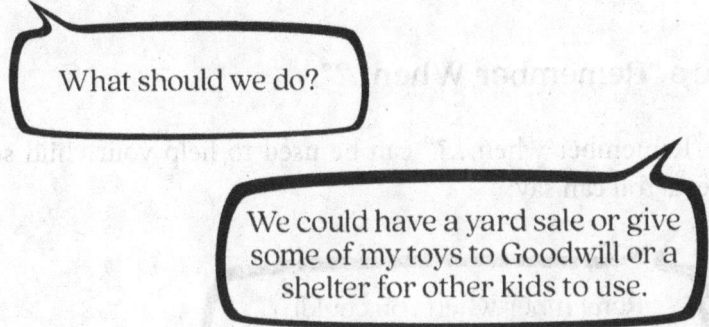

What should we do?

We could have a yard sale or give some of my toys to Goodwill or a shelter for other kids to use.

As ideas come up, parents can say if they are or aren't comfortable with them and why. Our kids might come up with an idea that we hadn't thought of but is a great solution to the problem.

Make a Wish

In wish-making, the child says something that isn't possible to do at that time and the parent rephrases it as a wish. When kids make a wish, it can even help them calm down.

It's getting dark, so we need to head home.

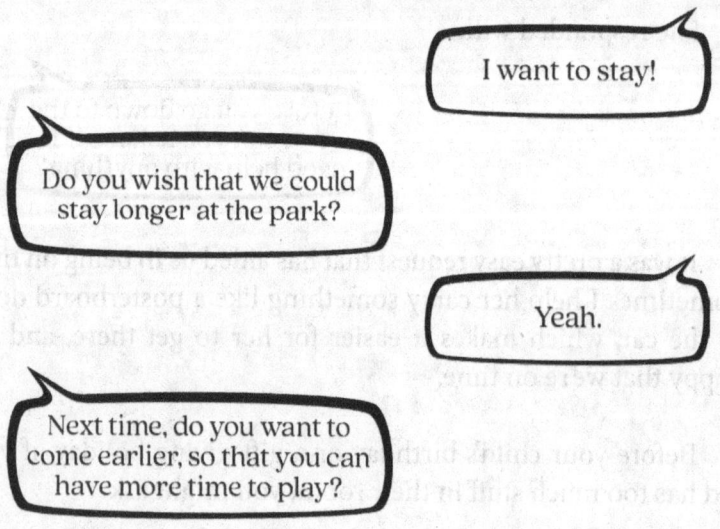

I want to stay!

Do you wish that we could stay longer at the park?

Yeah.

Next time, do you want to come earlier, so that you can have more time to play?

Use a "Remember When...?"

"Remember when...?" can be used to help your child self-reflect. You can say:

Remember when you couldn't reach the cabinet? Look at how much you've grown!

Remember when you looked at picture books? Now you can read chapter books!

This lets your children see how far they've come and be proud of their accomplishments.

Self-Reflect

Remember to self-reflect as a parent, to see all the progress you've made. You might think, "Things have really changed since my child started going to school. I have more time now and I'm grateful for that."

Or perhaps you ponder, "If my child had done that a few months ago I would have raised my voice, but I handled that better. I'm proud of myself."

You can also tell your child when you handle something well as a parent that had previously been hard for you. This shows your child that you aren't perfect, but you're working on improving. It's a good model for kids to see that if they want to, they can change and get better too.

Communication Tips

Tell your kids how you feel and why

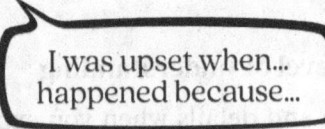

I was upset when... happened because...

Get down on their level when you speak with them

Imagine how it would feel if you were a small child and you had this big adult talking down to you. It might feel better to the child when you're at eye level.

Acknowledge their feelings

If your child loses a game, instead of saying they shouldn't feel sad or cry, be supportive.

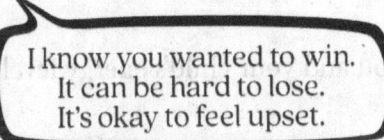

I know you wanted to win. It can be hard to lose. It's okay to feel upset.

Bring up one issue at a time

Try not to bring up things from the past, so that the other person doesn't get defensive. Avoid saying, "You always do *this*," or "You never do *that*."

No one likes to think that they *always* do anything!

Admit if you don't know something

It's okay to look things up. Teach this skill to your child.

Be honest

If you're open and honest with your kids, they will be with you too.

By being truthful and vulnerable, you're showing them that it's okay to make mistakes, and that you don't have to be perfect.

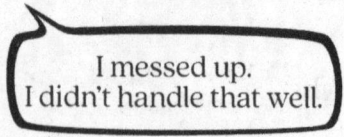

I messed up.
I didn't handle that well.

Consider your child's age and level of understanding

Use age-appropriate language and details when you explain things, like where babies come from.

Match your child's energy

If your child comes in super excited that they've found a slug, instead of saying, "Ew, gross," try to see that they're into it and say:

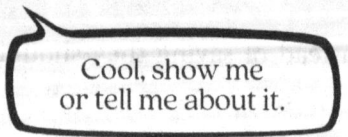

Cool, show me
or tell me about it.

Things go better when you and your child's energy levels are in sync.

Prepare your child for change

Give your child a few minutes' warning before it's time to go, so they can complete what they're working on.

When you tell your child what will come next and it does, they learn they can trust and can count on you.

> We're leaving in a few minutes.
> Finish up what you're playing
> and then we'll say goodbye.

Timing matters

It may not be the best time to have a tough conversation if we, or our kids, are hungry or tired.

Ask:

> Do you want me to help you
> fix this or do you want me
> to just listen?

Your child may not want you to solve the problem. They may just need you to listen and say you understand how they're feeling, and that it will be okay.[10]

Effective communication with our kids takes effort and practice. We won't be perfect and we will make mistakes. But if our kids see us trying to communicate and attempting to improve, we'll have a closer, more positive relationship with them.

Communicating with Neurodivergent Children

I know firsthand the challenges and the highs of parenting a neurodivergent child. I have tried to include research showcasing the voices of neurodivergent authors and those with neurodivergent children.

Neurodivergent and neurotypical people have a difference in how their brains work.

Emily Kircher-Morris[11] is a mental health counselor, neurodivergent person, and parent of neurodiverse kids. She explains that one way of thinking is not right or wrong and does not need to be fixed or cured.

Parents of neurodivergent kids may feel a great deal of stress, worry, and like there is a never-ending list of things to do. They may think parents of neurotypical kids can't fully understand what it's like for them.[12]

It's common for parents of neurodivergent children to criticize themselves for how they've acted and feel guilty, inadequate, and ashamed. The solution is self-compassion.[13]

Remind yourself that this happens to everyone and that you're doing the best you can in each moment.

 Action: Pause your reading and say to yourself, "It's okay to feel this way. It's okay to be in pain. It's okay to be upset."

Doing this calms your nervous system so you can respond in a better way. (See Chapter 1 for more on self-compassion.)

Neurodivergent children want to communicate and they're trying hard to do so, but it might be tough for them to understand our thoughts and feelings, and to know what to say or do.

It can also be difficult for us as parents to understand them. We can listen and acknowledge their feelings, try to see things from their perspective, have compassion and empathy for them and for us, notice how hard they are trying to communicate, and remember that they are probably doing the best they can too.

Tips for Communicating with Neurodivergent Kids

Be patient, slow, and direct

Let them know they can ask you questions. Try to be flexible if your child is having a hard time adjusting to a new situation.

Brainstorm solutions

Work with your child and ask them questions.

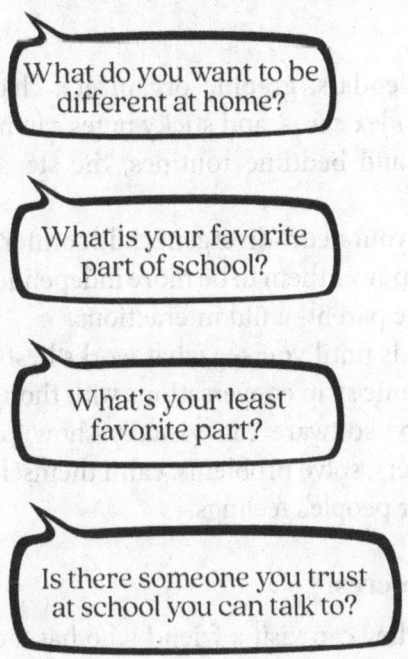

What do you want to be different at home?

What is your favorite part of school?

What's your least favorite part?

Is there someone you trust at school you can talk to?

By collaborating with your child on solutions to problems, you increase their motivation to be involved in the solution.

Conversations are like a ping-pong game

A good conversation is never one-sided. Instead, a conversation is like a ping-pong game, with one person hitting the ball over the net, then waiting for the other person to return it.

Talk with your child about what it means to be a friend. Friends are kind; they take turns, help you when you need it, and ask about your interests. You can read books and watch TV shows and movies about emotions and friendship.

Role-play

Practice conversations, such as what will happen on the first day of school, how to ask a friend to play, and how to talk to a teacher.

Use visual aids

Using tools such as calendars, graphic organizers, charts, diagrams, checklists, 3 x 5 index cards, and sticky notes can help your child learn morning and bedtime routines, the steps of a chore, and social skills.

Visual supports can give your neurodivergent child comfort in knowing what to expect, empower them to be more independent, and encourage more positive parent–child interactions.

Try out different methods until you see what works best for your child. Social stories, comic strip conversations with thought bubbles, and digital apps or software can visually show your child how to act around others, solve problems, calm themselves down, and understand other people's feelings.

Encourage their special interest

If your child likes cats, they can visit a friend who has a cat, you can go together to a cat café, or once old enough, they could volunteer at a pet shelter.

If your kid likes trains, you can take them to a train museum, or you may encourage them to help plan a family vacation in which you take trains for part of it.

If your child likes computers, you can enroll them in an online class, such as at Outschool, or in a camp on robotics.

Discuss that other people may or may not want to hear about their special interest, or that sometimes it just isn't the right time, such as during a math class.

In my family we say "time and place" to each other when someone is saying something inappropriate. We don't take offense because we've all been told it.

Suggest that your child join groups and take part in hobbies that have to do with their special interest, where they might make friends. Having a mentor, role model, teacher, or public figure who is similar to your child can be helpful too.

Help your child label their feelings

Give your child words to describe how they are feeling, such as happy, frustrated, excited, or anxious. Then validate those emotions so your child feels understood.

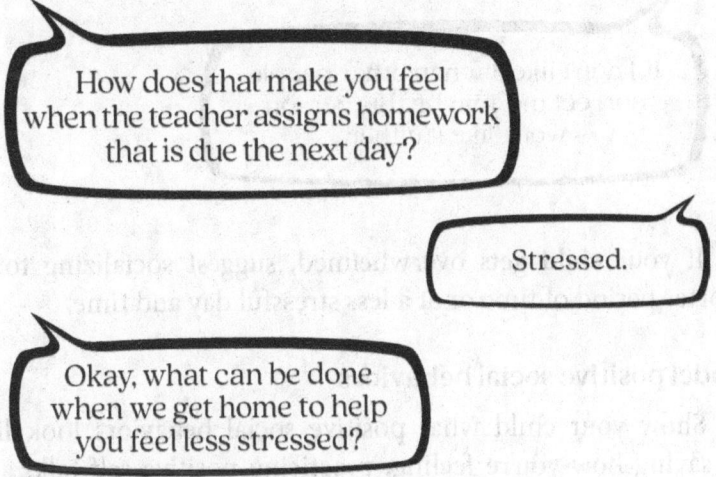

How does that make you feel when the teacher assigns homework that is due the next day?

Stressed.

Okay, what can be done when we get home to help you feel less stressed?

Don't force eye contact

Some neurodivergent people say it's easier to focus on another person's words if they don't also have to stress about looking them in the eyes. So don't force eye contact if your child isn't comfortable with it.

Encourage your child to take a pause

Taking a pause before stating their opinions gives your child the opportunity to ask themselves:

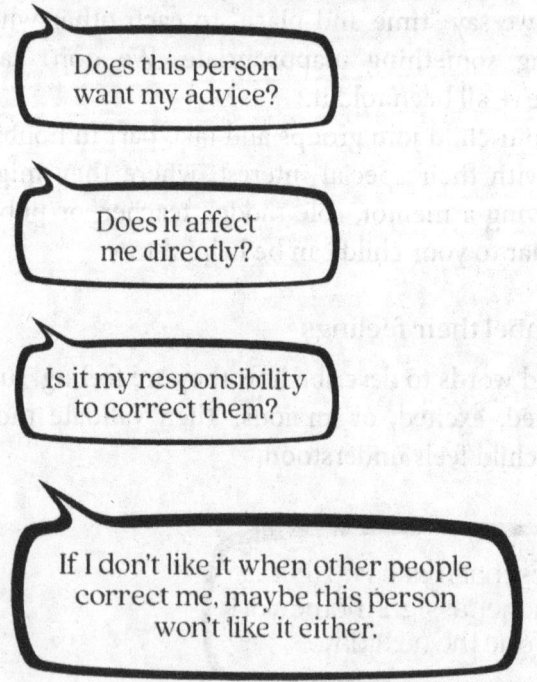

Does this person want my advice?

Does it affect me directly?

Is it my responsibility to correct them?

If I don't like it when other people correct me, maybe this person won't like it either.

If your child gets overwhelmed, suggest socializing for a shorter period of time or at a less stressful day and time.

Model positive social behaviors

Show your child what positive social behaviors look like by saying how you're feeling, practicing positive self-talk, and admitting to your mistakes. Discuss your child's strengths and challenges, explaining that everybody has both.

In kindergarten, my child came home upset that another girl in her class was reading chapter books and she wasn't yet. I talked to her about it.

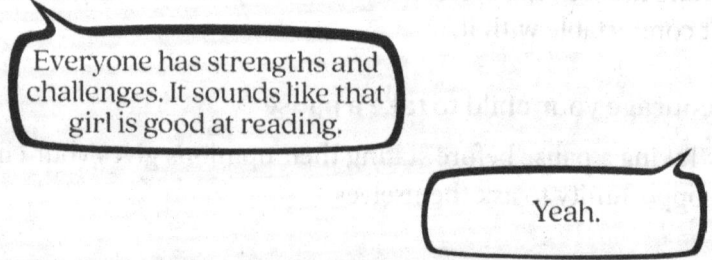

Everyone has strengths and challenges. It sounds like that girl is good at reading.

Yeah.

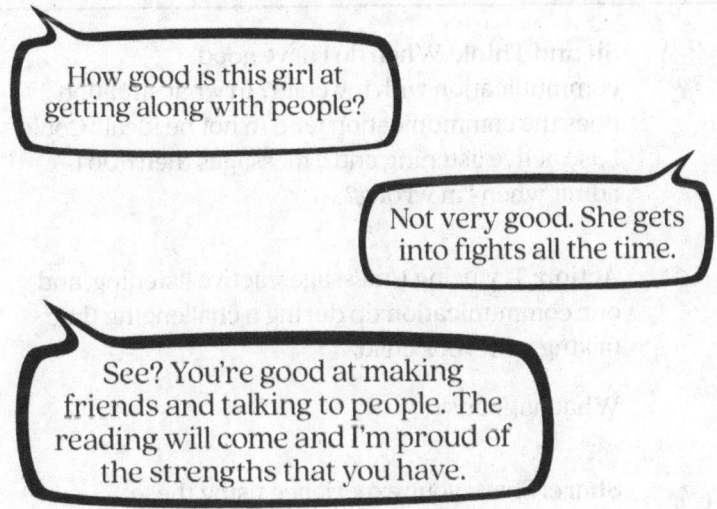

How good is this girl at getting along with people?

Not very good. She gets into fights all the time.

See? You're good at making friends and talking to people. The reading will come and I'm proud of the strengths that you have.

Find support in your community

Meeting others who have similar challenges and wins can help you feel less alone and can benefit your well-being. It's crucial for neurodiverse families to find a place where they feel accepted and understood, and to be able to connect with others.

Find professionals who get it

These professionals have empathy, are flexible, and are able to listen and ask why, instead of simply judging and labeling behaviors.

Speech and language therapy, social skills training, occupational therapy, drama classes, art and music therapy, and individual therapy may be of help, depending on the child. The earlier the better for interventions.[14]

We want to have open, healthy communication with our neurodivergent kids so that we can better understand how they're feeling, and to determine if they need more support at home or at school.

As parents, we want to brainstorm ideas with them and have discussions. We can also help them learn how to ask for help and how to advocate for themselves.

Sit and Think: When do I have good communication with my child? In what situation does the communication tend to not be ideal? Could I use active listening and I-messages then? Do I admit when I'm wrong?

Action: Try using I-messages, active listening, and one communication tip during a challenging time talking with your child.

What happens?

Share: Share your experience using these communication tools on your socials with #ParentingWithSelfCompassion or at DrJenFerris.com.

Just as communication tips are important with our kids, so too is discipline. But what even is discipline?

Chapter 10

Discipline: It May Not Mean What You Think It Means

(Yes, That's a *Princess Bride* Reference)

"Always obey your parents—when they are present."
Mark Twain

O nce I stole some candy from a small convenience store and when my dad found out, he took me back there. On the way, he explained to me *why* it was important not to steal.

> The man who owns the store needs us to pay for his goods so he can stay in business, and it's wrong to steal. Would you want someone to go into your bedroom and take something?

"No," I replied, staring at the ground. I returned the candy, apologized and meant it, because I understood why the behavior wasn't okay.

Disciplining kids is tough. There is judgment and criticism from others and from ourselves that we're doing things wrong. You'll likely make some mistakes, and you won't be alone. No one is perfect. A good place to start is by learning what discipline is—and what it is not.

The Difference Between Discipline and Punishment

Discipline

Ken Ginsburg[1] describes the purpose of discipline as teaching children how to behave in society. The goal of discipline is for our kids to internalize right from wrong and to have self-control, so they'll make good choices in the future, when we aren't there.

We want our children to become well-adjusted, independent adults, who are kind and can contribute to society.

Punishment

According to author and lecturer Alfie Kohn,[2] when a child does something wrong and is given a penalty, or has a toy or privilege taken away, that's a punishment. Typical punishments are spankings, time-outs, groundings, and the taking away of electronics.

While these seem to work in the short-term because the child stops doing the unwanted behavior, they don't work well in the long-term, and there are often more unwanted behaviors to come.

With punishments, children don't learn why they should do the right thing. Ultimately, punishment only teaches kids to avoid getting punished.

Children who are frequently punished may also start to feel worse about themselves, as they start to believe that they must be bad if people keep doing unkind things to them.

If a teen thinks a grounding is unfair, they may rebel against it and sneak out of the house. People don't like to be controlled and will only put up with it for so long before resentment and anger build, and they'll want to assert their independence.[3] When adults use punishments often, it hurts their relationship with their child.[4]

The Issue with Spanking

When my dad held me down and spanked me, I felt angry and powerless. I remember how I felt in that moment, but I don't remember what I had done wrong.

The American Academy of Pediatrics[5] and the majority of US pediatricians (74 percent)[6] recommend that parents don't spank their children. Although fewer parents support spanking than in the past, many parents in the US and around the world still spank their kids.

Spanking or smacking teaches children that it's okay to hit someone you love and that it's a good way to solve problems in a relationship. The resentment the child feels toward the parent who spanks can stay with them for years to come.

In children, spanking increases aggression, lowers self-esteem, and is connected to more depression and anxiety, drug use, delinquency, antisocial behavior, lower vocabulary scores, and poorer mental health.

Hitting, yelling at, and shaming kids can raise their stress hormones and lead to changes in their brains. Spanking can also harm the parent's relationship with the child, as there tend to be more power struggles, fear, and resentment.[7]

Bandura's Bobo doll experiment[8] revealed that children will imitate the behavior they see an adult perform, especially if the adult is of the same gender. It showed how when kids see adults model aggression, they are more likely to become aggressive themselves. If you're interested, you can go to YouTube and search for "Bandura and Bobo doll experiment."

You can also find the 20/20 episode about spanking titled, "A Lesson They Will Never Forget" on YouTube.

Okay, so we try to not hit our kids, but then time-outs are fine, right?

Time-Outs

Time-outs are when, after an undesired behavior, parents take their kid to another area for the child to calm down and think about what they did wrong. The rule of thumb is one minute of time-out for every year of the child's age, so time-outs would last three minutes for 3-year-olds and five minutes for 5-year-olds.[9]

While time-outs do take children away from the area of the misbehavior, and they might calm down over time, these kids are probably not thinking about what they did wrong, and they may not understand why they have been sent away. Children put in time-out are more likely thinking about how they feel angry at and rejected by the person who put them there.

> *Kids who are often put in time-out feel isolated, lonely, and abandoned.*

Their self-esteem and self-confidence starts to decrease, which makes for more bad behavior, and can lead to mental health problems, like depression and anxiety.[10]

> *You and your kids aren't enemies—you're on the same team.*

When your children behave in a way that you dislike, instead of sending them away, keep them nearby.

Hold them and say:

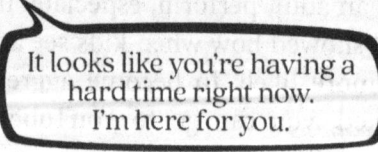

It looks like you're having a hard time right now. I'm here for you.

They can express their feelings safely, and you being there with them also builds trust.

When they're ready, you can discuss the undesired behavior, the feelings involved, and how to handle it better next time.

If punishment isn't great, then what can parents do instead? Rewards, right?

Rewards

A reward is something of value that's promised to a child for good behavior. Rewards can be a sweet treat, a sticker, toys, a gold star, money, or a privilege like extra television or device time.

Like punishments, rewards might work in the short-term, but they aren't effective at improving kids' behavior long-term.

The more kids are rewarded, the more they stop taking creative risks.

They'll do a task less well and lose interest in the task.

They think, "If my parents have to bribe me to do this, it must be something that I don't want to do."

When kids are intrinsically (internally) motivated, they do things because they want to, for their own enjoyment. They color, read, and share because they choose to, and it makes them feel good.

This is different from kids being extrinsically (externally) motivated to do something. Are you reading a book because you want to find out what happens or because you're trying to get a pizza or sticker?

Ultimately, we want kids to do the right thing because it's the right thing to do, not because they're being bribed in some way. The bribes won't always be there, and they'll still have to choose how to act.

To minimize the downsides of rewards, parents can offer the reward as a surprise after the desired behavior. You can make rewards similar to the task, such as getting a new book for finishing reading a book. Parents can give children as much choice in the reward as possible.[11]

Another type of reward is praise.

Praise

Praise is a verbal reward that parents give about their child's appearance, behavior, characteristics, or accomplishments, to try to change the child's behavior.

Praise seems great but there are some downsides. Children can get hooked on praise, wanting or needing this external validation, even into adulthood.

They might start asking, "Is this good? Did I do this right?" And then they can become adults who need constant reassurance.

When you say, "Good girl" or "Good boy," it implies a moral judgment, and the child might feel like if they don't behave well, or look the way you want, then they are "bad."

To decrease the harm of praise, parents can say they liked the behavior, not the child, and be as specific as possible. Instead of saying, "Good job" when your child draws a picture, you can say:

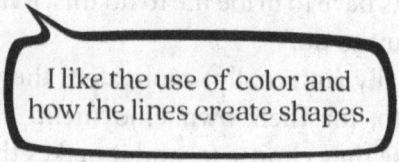

I like the use of color and how the lines create shapes.

If you like what your child is doing and you want to respond but you don't want to praise, you can instead:[12]

Describe what you see

Your child will see that you noticed their behavior, but you aren't judging them.

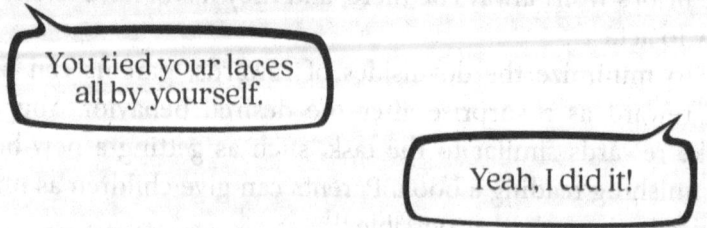

You tied your laces all by yourself.

Yeah, I did it!

You can also describe the effect your child's actions had on another person:

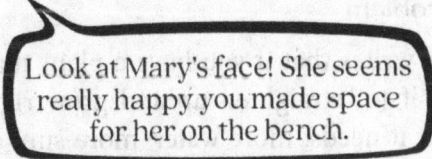

Look at Mary's face! She seems really happy you made space for her on the bench.

Ask your child questions

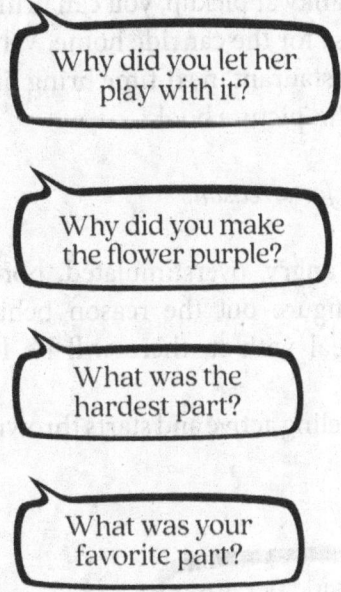

Why did you let her play with it?

Why did you make the flower purple?

What was the hardest part?

What was your favorite part?

What might be some discipline strategies that could be more successful in the long-term than punishments and rewards?

What to Do Instead

Discipline techniques have been sprinkled throughout this book. Giving your child choices (Chapter 6), picking and choosing your battles (Chapter 7), and using active listening and I-messages (Chapter 9) are all things you can do as a parent to help prevent meltdowns, tantrums, and arguments from ever happening in the first place. Here are some additional strategies.

Get to the root of the problem

Dr. Laura Markham[13] writes that if you have a plant that is drooping, do you yell at it to "straighten up and grow right!" or do you figure out what it needs: more water, more sun, or a bigger pot?

The same is true for your kids. Try to figure out the deeper reasons for your child's behavior.

If your child is hungry and cranky at pickup, you can bring a snack like grapes and string cheese for the car ride home. When you see your child is bored at a restaurant, next time bring little toys, coloring, a maze, or a find-the-picture book.

Kids misbehave for a reason.

They may be tired, hungry, angry, overstimulated, bored, or feeling ignored. When you figure out the reason behind their unwanted behavior and deal with it, there will be less problem behavior.

For example, when a child is feeling active and starts throwing things in the living room:

> You can't throw the ball inside because the lamp might get broken, but you can throw it outside. Let's go out, I'll play catch with you.

Discuss and explain

One night when I was seven years old, my parents said, "Go to sleep," and because I was *that* kid, I responded with:

> You can make me go to bed, but you can't make me go to sleep!

And while I was technically right, I lay in bed for as long as possible, trying to stay awake, and seething with anger. Maybe a little explanation about why sleep was important would have helped.

Another night, I woke up in the middle of the night and my dad said I could play quietly with LEGO bricks until I was tired. I did that, got tired, and went back to sleep. There was much less drama, and I remember it because of how reasonable it had seemed.

We can't expect our kids to just do what we say because we say so.

Kids, like adults, deserve explanations.

During a discussion, you can squat down to your child's eye level and talk about what happened. Did their behavior hurt someone?

> It's not okay to pinch because that hurts him.

If there's a safety reason a child shouldn't be doing something, like running in the street or climbing on flimsy furniture that could tip over, then explain that. Your child will understand and be less likely to do it in the future.

> Running out in the street is not okay. It isn't safe and you could get hurt.

If there isn't a good reason why they can't do something, then it might be time to think about whether or not it's a good rule.

Be honest with your kids. Explain why. This makes acceptance more likely and the next time this comes up, it might be easier.

Our child's feelings are always okay to have, but their behaviors may not be acceptable. For instance:

> It's fine to feel angry when Charlie takes the toy you're playing with, Esmerelda, but it's not okay to hit him.

If it's biting, you can say:

> That hurt, Randolph. It's not okay to bite people. If you want to bite something, you can bite on this teething ring or washcloth.

Talk with your child about the different ways to respond in a conflict and what would be preferred by both of you.

Give natural and logical consequences

Natural consequences are things that happen automatically because of a child's actions. Through natural consequences children can learn critical thinking skills.

A child goes outside without their jacket; they get cold and go back in to get it. A boy leaves his LEGO bricks out, steps on one, and feels some mild pain. He might decide to clean up his toys.[14]

Logical consequences are when the adult imposes something on the child that relates to the child's misbehavior. The adult's response makes logical sense.

If a child makes a mess, they have to help clean it up. When a boy breaks his sister's toy, the parent says he either has to help fix it or pay for a replacement out of his own allowance.[15]

These consequences are put in place by the child's parents, but they relate to the misbehavior and are appropriate for the child's age.

If your child says something you don't like and you take away their electronics, that doesn't make sense; they aren't connected. Just like you'd want reprimands at work to make sense, your child wants things to seem fair and consistent too.

Give a warning

A few minutes before you leave a birthday party, you let your kids know:

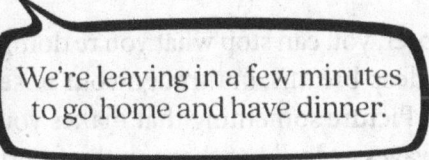

We're leaving in a few minutes to go home and have dinner.

Then after a couple of minutes, you tell them:

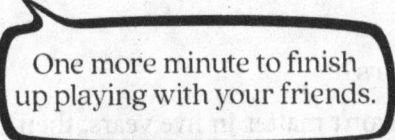

One more minute to finish up playing with your friends.

Then when it's time to go, you can do something fun like:

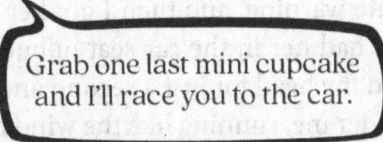

Grab one last mini cupcake and I'll race you to the car.

Take a parent time-out

When you're feeling angry and overwhelmed, make sure your children are safe and take a parent time-out. Go to a quiet place and take some deep breaths. If you can calm yourself down, then you'll be less likely to say or do something you may regret later.

Having a break can help you figure out how you're feeling, why, and how to explain some of that when you go back in with your child. You can also use the quiet time to think about why your kid may have acted that way. You'll be more patient and supportive when you talk with your child.

Breathe in. Breathe out. I am safe.
I am calm for my child.

Even just pausing for a few seconds can be a huge help.

Hit the pause button

When you're really upset, you can stop what you're doing and breathe—just a few slow, deep breaths, in through your nose and out through your mouth. Picture something that makes you feel calm, such as the ocean waves or walking through the forest.

Say to yourself, "This is *not* an emergency. It will be okay." This quick moment of pause can help you respond to your child with more care.

Will this matter in five years?

The 5 x 5 rule says if it won't matter in five years, then don't spend more than five minutes worrying about it now.[16]

Once I was with my young preschooler at the park, and we had to leave to get my older child from school. I gave her a five-minute warning, a one-minute warning, and then I got her into the car. She was squirming. I had her in the car seat unbuckled when I heard a noise. I turned my head for just a second and she quickly slithered out from under me, running like the wind back to the park.

I ran after my three-year-old. I had to pick her up, kicking and screaming, put her back in the car seat, hold her down, and buckle her in. I let out an "Ah!" Then I turned back to her and, as calmly as I could muster, I said:

> I see that you're upset. You want to stay longer. I'm sorry, but we have to get your sister from school.

As I sat in the driver's seat upset, I tried to calm down. I asked myself, "Will this matter in five years?" No. I knew I had done the right thing. I took some deep breaths, calmed down, and drove off.

Be predictable and follow through

Children do better when their parents are predictable in their discipline and routines, so their kids know what to expect and feel secure. If you allow something one time and not the next, treat siblings differently, or don't follow through with the things you say you're going to do, it's confusing and it doesn't seem right to them.

When children can't predict their parents' behaviors, it can lead to anxiety and even hostility.[17] Sometimes, things have to change with the schedule; just let your kids know why.

> We have to get up early tomorrow, so let's head to bed and read for a bit.

> Usually your bedtime is 8 p.m. but since it's a vacation, you can stay up to 9 p.m. if you want.

Model the behavior you want to see

You know the saying, "Do as I say, not as I do?" Yeah, that doesn't work.

Children watch their parents and learn from their example. When we clear our dishes, they're more likely to do the same. But if we swear and we tell them not to swear, it probably won't work.

Let's try to act the way we want our children to behave, by saying please and thank you, being hard-working, kind, helpful, sharing with others, and trying to stay calm and patient when we're frustrated.

You won't be able to model amazing behaviors all the time—like when you're going on four hours' sleep and your toddler has a million questions. Acknowledge that you could have responded to that last question better, take a deep breath, and say how you'll do it better next time. When your children see that you're not beating yourself up and you're trying to improve, they will learn to be gentle with themselves too.

Use foreshadowing

By the time your kids get to be, say, 8 years old, you'll know them quite well. Not only will they have your genes, but you'll have spent many hours with them. In fact, you'll be able to predict what they're going to say in response to your comments.

This is actually a superpower. I've had full-on conversations with my children in my head, only to decide to keep my mouth shut because it wasn't going to benefit me or them to say what I was about to say. If you can take a second to mentally run the conversation in your mind, then you can actually reduce problems like talking back, complaining, whining, and temper tantrums.

Now all those quiet moments with my parents during a car ride or in the kitchen make sense. They knew when to shut up and be quiet, so that I wouldn't make things worse when I responded to them. Thanks Mom and Dad. I know I was a handful.

Prevent problems before they occur

Every once in a while when my younger child was little, we would go to a restaurant where they didn't have any children's menus to color on, and it always felt like a long time waiting for the food to come. So, I had to get creative.

I would bring a bag of board books and other little toys. After the bag was done and the food had still not arrived, we would play with the cloth napkins.

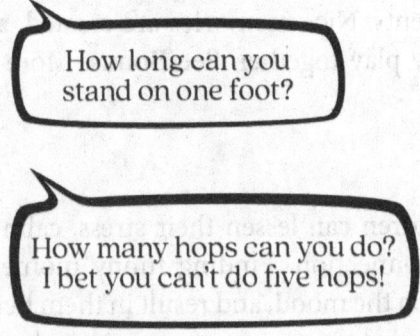

> What shapes can you make with the napkin? A circle? Triangle? Square? Diamond? Oval? Star?

You can keep an activity bag like this in your car to grab before appointments and change what's in it as your kids get older.

Turn it into a game

Getting creative and thinking of little games while waiting with your child can help pass the time more quickly and prevent meltdowns due to boredom.

When we had to wait in the doctor's office and there weren't any toys, I would challenge my children to games of Rock, Paper, Scissors, I-Spy, or I'd ask them:

> How long can you stand on one foot?

> How many hops can you do? I bet you can't do five hops!

Likewise, you can create your own games to make eating time and brushing teeth as fun as possible, like an airplane or train going into their mouth and across the teeth. "Vroom." And make up your own games that seem fun to you and your little one.

It's time to play

In her book *Raising Good Humans*, mindfulness mentor and coach, Hunter Clarke-Fields,[18] writes that, "Play is the currency of childhood. Children need to play like they need air and water."

Through play, children learn how to take turns, share, get along with others and cooperate, how to regulate their emotions, build self-control, have empathy, and be a good friend and person.

Kids develop patience and learn how to handle frustration. During play they become curious and creative, practice using language, improve their physical development, and learn math and science skills.

By playing, children improve their problem-solving and negotiation skills, become independent, confident, and they build better leadership skills, such as how to make decisions and speak up for themselves.

*Through play, kids come to understand themselves
and the world.*

Children will open up about their thoughts and feelings during play with their parents. Nice memories are created, and both feel closer when they play together. See Bonus: More on Play for more play ideas.

Use humor

Using humor with children can lessen their stress, calm us down, and improve our connection. Finding funny moments can surprise our kids, lighten the mood, and result in them being more cooperative. It also reduces our own stress and makes us feel happier.[19]

Exaggerate what's happening. Use reverse psychology by saying:

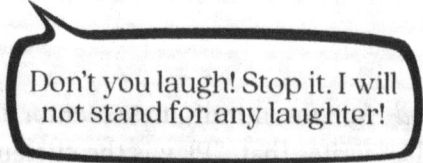

Don't you laugh! Stop it. I will not stand for any laughter!

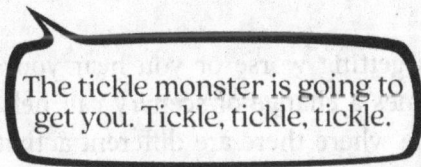

The tickle monster is going to get you. Tickle, tickle, tickle.

Make a funny face, sing a silly song, tell a knock knock joke:

> *Knock, knock.*
> *Who's there?*
> *Dwayne.*
> *Dwayne who?*
> *Dwayne the bathtub—I'm drowning!*

You can fake like you're falling down, talk for the dog, pretend stuffed animals are alive, and make fun of yourself:

I bet my hair looks crazy right now? Do I look like an alien?

As parents, we can use humor with our kids to defuse a difficult situation. If you're sitting down to talk with your child about not doing their chores, you can do an impression of how you must sound when you're being serious.

When you and your child are laughing, it makes things less tense and the conversation can go more smoothly.

Discipline Tips

Avoid power struggles

When your pre-teen says, "You just don't get it, that's not how it works," just say, "Okay," and walk away. You don't have to get into a debate about every little thing. Sometimes, peace in the house is more important.

Move to a new setting

If a child's behavior is getting worse or you hear yourself saying, "No," a lot, sometimes a change of scenery can help. If it's safe to do so, go outside where there are different activities to choose from, like sand, water, chalk, hopscotch, climbing, running, ball play, or go for a walk.

Have fewer rules

Rules for safety, privacy, or to protect people's property are fine, but that's about it.

You don't need to have a million rules. Too many rules can be stressful for parents to keep track of and enforce, and they can hurt kids' creativity and spontaneity. Remember that you and your child are on the same team.

Be honest with your children when you make a mistake

I messed up.
I didn't handle that well.

By being truthful, you are showing them that it's okay to make mistakes.

Celebrate the small wins

We don't tend to remember our great parenting moments as much as we remember the things that go wrong. Say some nice things to yourself when you do something well or when things go right with your kids.

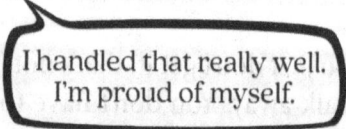

I handled that really well.
I'm proud of myself.

Make sure to give yourself breaks and focus on what you can control. Try to be patient when your child is taking a long time getting ready in the morning.

When you're able to think, "This is not that big a deal; it's just one day," you'll be more likely to stay calm and not raise your voice.

It can help to keep an accurate, big picture perspective. Being late to school once, or having a messy room occasionally, is not the end of the world. Happiness and harmony in the home matters too.

If your child's behaviors are challenging and you're having a hard time, remind yourself that you're not the only one.

Find other parents who are going through similar things and seek out outside services as needed.

Tips for Disciplining Neurodivergent Kids

Disciplining your children when you and they think differently can be challenging. For your neurodivergent children, social rules may not make sense, they may get overwhelmed, and they can feel like they're doing things wrong.

Here are some tips.

Have consistent, predictable routines

Having routines can let your neurodivergent child know what to expect and feel more in control.

If mornings are stressful, do as much as you can the night before, including getting your child's clothes out, their lunch made, and their school bag ready by the door. You can also try having a consistent bedtime routine that ends with reading in bed.

When things are predictable, it can help reduce your child's anxiety. If keeping track of time is a challenge, discuss the use of alarms, timers, reminders, or some other kind of external timekeeper.

Break down tasks into smaller steps

The actions involved in cleaning your child's room may include picking up dirty clothes, placing them in the hamper, putting toys away, and making the bed.

If cleaning their room is overwhelming, write the steps out and get containers with labels, so your child knows where each item goes. When your kids are successful at doing small tasks, they'll feel more confident and independent.

Pay attention to possible triggers

You may start to notice that certain places, people, or situations tend to upset your child, and that if you can adapt or avoid them, things go more smoothly.

If you're at a park, museum, or indoor playground and things seem too loud, bright, hot, or crowded, you can move to a quieter area, or decide to leave and come back at another time.

If the tags in your child's clothes bother them, they can be removed.

Talk with your kids about what might help them feel calmer. They know better than anyone if there's a sensory stimulation trigger that is the cause of them being upset.

Once you know the real cause of their discomfort, you can work with them on a solution. Sometimes, just changing the time of day can help. For example, after school let them have a break with a snack before doing homework. Just don't wait too long or they might get tired.

Adjust the home environment

You can get

- fidget toys
- earplugs or noise-canceling headphones
- a weighted blanket
- a swing
- a special cushion
- a squeeze or hug machine

- sensory toys like sand, water, finger paints, slime, Play-Doh
- puzzles
- books.

Even changing up the furniture in your home can reduce anxiety and make your child feel more comfortable. Every child is different so if something doesn't work, don't give up. Keep trying until you find something that works for you and your child.

Collaborate with your kids

Work together on issues in the home, involving your child in the discussion on topics that affect them. Brainstorm ideas to problems, without judgment, and pick one or two changes that you can both agree on.

For instance, instead of yelling in the morning to get to the car on time, there can be a timer and a two-minute warning.

If your child asks a question every few minutes while you work or relax at home, have them write down all of their questions, batching them together for a time when you're better able to answer them. If they can write, you can give them a journal, pad of paper, or an electronic device to write down their questions.

It can also be good to change up your expectations. Are there some tasks in the morning that can be done at a later time or not at all? When your child participates in solving problems, it makes it more likely that they'll cooperate.

Teach your child coping strategies

In times of stress, if your kids can be mindful, take breaks, count, and breathe in and out using slow, deep breaths, it may help them stay calm and have better responses. You can also model mindful breathing when you're feeling overwhelmed, such as when you're stuck in traffic.[20]

Remember that being a parent to a neurodivergent child is challenging work that requires a great deal of patience. Be kind to yourself when you make a mistake, and find ways to give yourself care and relaxation.

Have people you can talk to (friends and family, other parents, support groups, a therapist), as well as podcasts, blogs, and books that you listen to and read, and take part in your own hobbies and interests away from your child.

When you feel the most like yourself, you can be
the best parent to your child.

 Sit and Think: Do you currently use punishments and rewards in your parenting? How's that going?

Are there times when you could add a discussion or take a parent time-out to calm down?

Think of one specific issue and what could be at the root of the problem.

 Action: Try discussing a problem with your child or taking a parent time-out when you're upset. How did it go?

Try one of the discipline tips, such as noticing your parenting wins.

 Share: Share what happened when you discussed, took a parent time-out, or reflected on your parenting wins on your socials with #ParentingWithSelfCompassion or at DrJenFerris.com.

Changing how we discipline takes practice. Another area of parenthood to keep learning about is how to deal with children and electronics.

Chapter 11

Living in a Digital Age: Dealing with Electronics

"Technology makes it possible for people to gain control over everything, except over technology."

John Tudor

One summer, my uncle took his teenage grandsons to Europe. He was excited to check out colleges with them, to see if they might want to study abroad. But at the beginning of the trip, instead of looking around them, the teens had their faces in their screens.

The iPhone was first released into the wild in 2007,[1] which, in the scheme of things, isn't really that long ago.

Now, have I put my child in front of the TV to watch *Curious George* while I made a quick dinner? Sure. But you know what? That kid is still alive and turned out to be a pretty good person. Let's be kind and compassionate to each other and to ourselves.

Technology is just one tool that we have and there are many benefits to having our kids use digital devices.

Benefits to Technology

Technology connects people, allows them to communicate, and it can strengthen relationships. Kids can work on school projects together and talk about homework, relationships, and pop culture.

When we weren't able to go back home to visit our relatives during the holidays because of COVID, we could FaceTime, and my kids could still see and talk with their grandparents, aunts, and uncles.

Children can learn new words, languages, numbers, and develop analytical thinking and problem-solving skills.

They can improve their creativity, hand–eye coordination, and move their bodies.[2] Apps like Starfall, Duolingo, and Education can aid with these skills. Greenlight can be used to learn financial literacy.

Children can become computer literate, and by using programs like PowerPoint and Canva, they can learn skills that will set them up for success in future jobs.

My kids have made digital presentations and then shown them in front of the class. This can be good practice for a wide variety of jobs.

Kids can get involved in important causes, volunteer, raise awareness, and make the world a better place with the use of technology.

Children have made apps for anti-bullying (FaceUp.com), medication reminders (Pharm Alarm), and finding someone to sit with at lunch (Sit With Us).

But is it all good news?

Electronics Can Be Harmful When Used Too Much

Did Apple co-founder Steve Jobs give his kids iPhones and iPads because he loved his products so much and believed in them? Actually, no.

Steve Jobs, Bill Gates, Susan Wojcicki, Evan Spiegel, Alexis Ohanian, and Serena Williams have all talked about how they limit their kids' screen time, have digital curfews, and don't allow electronics at the dinner table.

Many of these giants in their field raise their kids mostly free of technology.[3] So why would these incredibly smart people not let their children play with the products that they helped to create?

There might just be some downsides to spending too much time using technology.

Note: While this book is aimed at parents of young children to pre-teens, kids are getting phones at younger and younger ages. I present the following information for you to have in your back pocket to make informed decisions about when and why to give your child a phone.

Downsides to Technology

By the age of 14, 91 percent of kids have a phone[4] and these teens can spend up to 11 hours a day on their devices.[5]

Teens, as well as adults, tend to underestimate how much they use their smartphones, checking their phones twice as much as they think they do.

Fifty percent of American teens report feeling addicted to their devices.[6]

Too much screen time is linked to[7]

- sleep problems, weight gain, high blood pressure, and diabetes
- decreased empathy and worse social skills
- less focus, a shorter attention span, and memory problems
- poorer grades
- lower self-esteem
- anxiety, stress, depression, loneliness, and isolation

- cyberbullying
- exposure to porn, online grooming, and possible predators
- body image issues, disordered eating, and suicidal thoughts.

Internet Gaming

Internet gaming can become a problem for kids and pre-teens when it negatively interferes with their lives.

In 2019, the World Health Organization (WHO) referred to this as "gaming disorder." Technology addiction is seen as a problem in Japan, China, and South Korea.[8]

If online gaming is out of control for someone you know, there are inpatient treatment centers such as reSTART in Washington and Reset in the US and Canada.

There are also support groups such as On-Line Gamers Anonymous (OLGA), Internet and Technology Addicts Anonymous (ITAA), Media Addicts Anonymous, and a section of ITAA for social media.

Resources for more information include Game Quitters and The Center for Humane Technology.

Media Guidelines

Because of these negatives, the American Academy of Pediatrics (AAP)[9] came up with media guidelines for parents.

Remember, these are just guidelines. So try to be forgiving of yourself if your kids go a little over.

- For infants up to 18 months old, zero screen time is advised, except for video chats with family. Instead, floor time with board books, rattles, mirrors, and other toys are good.

- For toddlers, 18 months to 2 years old, one hour per

day of screens is the most that's suggested. Watching high-quality, educational programs with a caregiver is recommended. Find an age-appropriate show that you're okay with like *Bluey*, *Sesame Street*, or *Barney*.

- For preschoolers, 2 to 5 years old, watching one hour or less on the weekdays and two hours or less on the weekends is preferred. It's ideal to watch educational shows together, like *Curious George*, *Daniel Tiger's Neighborhood*, *Thomas & Friends*, *Wonder Pets*, and *Dinosaur Train*.

- For school-age kids, 6 and older, and for teens, the aim is less than two hours of screen time a day of shows like *Bill Nye the Science Guy*, *Percy Jackson*, and *Survivor*. Physical movement, getting a good night's sleep, and having family meals together are encouraged.

Two hours of screen time or less is ideal but it doesn't always happen that way, especially when kids are on breaks from school.

Do your best at planning activities out of the house, monitoring electronics use and content, and then be forgiving if your child goes over a bit.

They can still grow up to be a good person, which is really what matters. And be kind to yourself—always.

When is the Right Time to Get a Phone?

Try to put off giving your child a phone for as long as possible. Then, it's recommended to do it between the ages of 10 and 14[10], when your child needs to be able to get in touch with you, and when they are responsible enough to have a phone, i.e., they won't immediately lose it or use it to cyberbully other kids.

Ask your child why they want a phone. All of the other kids having a phone is not a good enough reason.

Before you give your kid a phone, I'd suggest watching the documentary *Screenagers* with them.

If you're interested, there's a group of parents who take a pledge online and offer each other support in waiting to give their kids phones until eighth grade.

Social Awakening is a group that promotes healthy use of technology and social media.

Talk to your kids about some of the topics included in the Don't Press Send pledge, such as not posting something that you wouldn't say to that person's face.

When it's time, try not to start with a smartphone that has unlimited access to the internet. Start slow, with a device that lets your child text with friends. Just be ready to get texts from your kid with a million emojis!

Technology Tips

Have parental controls on

You can use apps such as Mobicip, Net Nanny, Bark, BrightCanary, and Qustodio.com.

Be present during screen use

If possible, have a computer in the shared family space for homework.

Prioritize

Suggest homework first and then technology time.

Take breaks

Encourage your kids to take breaks from electronics, and to delete or cut back on anything online that causes them stress. Turn off all notifications, and let mealtimes be tech-free.

Make an offline list of things to do away from technology. Items for this can include going for a walk, playing at the park, coloring with chalk, blowing bubbles, splashing in water, reading, dancing, visiting grandparents, cooking a new dish, having a family game night, playing with animals, and seeing friends.

Model what you want to see

Model good technology behaviors. Children tend to follow their parents' example when it comes to screen use. If you don't want your kids on their phones at the dinner table, stay off yours too.

Be proactive

Preview and watch TV shows and movies, and play video games with your kids. Take part in movie nights at home. To find what ages are appropriate, you can go to Common Sense Media, and for video game and app ratings you can go to the Entertainment Software Rating Board (ESRB).

Talk to your kids about technology

- Describe how it's designed to be addictive, with likes and endless scrolling.
- Inform your children that anything they post online can be seen by college admissions and future employers.
- Tell your kids not to share their personal information online, such as their address, school, passwords, and current location.
- Explain how to block and report harassing texts, and what to do if they experience cyberbullying, sexting, or online predators.
- Let them know to never give, send, or share sexually explicit images, and if they get sent one, to delete it immediately. In some US states, it's a felony to send or receive sexts. You can look up the sexting laws in your location.

Get everyone involved in using shared digital tools

As your kids get older they can get more involved in a shared family Google calendar, where they can add in their sporting events, friend get-togethers, play rehearsals, and other activities like dances, or when they'll be gone for part-time jobs.

Get consent

Ask your children's permission before sharing a picture of them online. (I got my children's consent for the pictures in this book.)[11]

We can help our kids practice how to search online and find valid information from multiple, credible sources, instead of taking misinformation at face value.

We can raise upstanders, who will take action when they see something that's wrong or harmful to others.

Please remember, with electronics, to be kind to yourself. If you let your child have an iPad in the car on a long trip to watch a movie, and they go over their two hours by a bit, it's not the end of the world.

They will survive and you are still a good parent.

Reading on Screens Versus on Paper

Research shows that if you read on paper, you'll understand and retain more of what you read, as opposed to reading on a screen.

People tend to read faster and skim more on devices and miss details.

Studies have found that students think they're learning more by reading on screens, but when tested, they aren't. LED screens can also make our brains more tired.[12]

Reading on screens is here to stay and there are some benefits. It's often cheaper and easier to access, such as getting audiobooks online and e-books for free through your local library.

It's better for the environment to read on screens, rather than printing out thousands of books. There can be links inserted into digital readings that make additional learning easier.

You can also adjust the size of the letters, the background color, and the typeface, for those with reading challenges. There's a typeface called Open Dyslexic, for people with dyslexia, to make reading easier.

There are many benefits to online reading, but to retain information, experts suggest slowing down and printing out anything that you really need to learn. Teens and adults can consider the situation when deciding which way to read.[13]

Digital Mindfulness

If mindfulness means being aware of your thoughts and feelings in the present moment without judgment, then digital mindfulness is about being present and intentional in your use of technology.[14] It's choosing how often you go on the internet and being aware of your online behaviors and posts.

> *The goal is to use technology in a mindful way*
> *that leads to more happiness, more productivity,*
> *and less stress and anxiety.*

As parents, when we are mindful with our online activities, our kids notice and are more likely to be conscious with their digital lives too.

> *Technology is neither good nor bad—it's just*
> *a tool. It is how we use it, and how it makes*
> *us and others feel that matters.*

To become more digitally mindful, ask yourself questions such as:
"How much time do I want to spend on social media, responding to emails, and checking the news each day?"

When you're online, check in with yourself and ask:
"How am I feeling?"
"Am I stressed or relaxed?"

If you feel like you're going online and checking social media too often, you can delete the most problematic apps from your phone. You'll still be able to go to those websites on your laptop, but this extra step makes it harder, and means that you'll be less likely to do it. If you're feeling distracted and unable to focus, you can install apps like the Freedom app to block websites, apps, or the entire internet. You can also check your total screen time at the end of the day or week.[15]

Notice your children during and after being online. Are they having fun or are they stressed out? Is technology helping or hurting their friendships? If something isn't working, involve your kids in working out a solution.

 Sit and Think: Am I using a device when my child is nearby? How often is my child using electronics? Do I ever watch or preview my kids' TV, movies, and video games? Do I feel like there's a healthy balance in my home with play and technology?

 Action: Try tracking how many hours you and your child use technology each day. Is it more on weekdays or weekends? Is it where you want it to be?

Watch a show with your child and talk with them about it. If you're at the park or somewhere else with your child, see if you can just be there and not on your phone.

 Share: Share your experience tracking your use of technology, watching and talking about a show with your child, and being present while playing with your child on your socials with #ParentingWithSelfCompassion or at DrJenFerris.com.

While being digitally mindful is important, it's also crucial to prioritize self-care, so that you don't burn out. This will help you to be the best possible parent for your child.

Chapter 12

Self-Care Isn't Selfish

"Self-care is how you take your power back."

Lalah Delia

Self-care is taking the time to do things that are healthy for you physically, mentally, and emotionally. It doesn't have to be big or cost a ton of money. Small things can be beneficial, like using a soap you like the smell of.

When choosing self-care activities, look for the ones that help you feel cared for and pampered, and that bring relaxation, joy, and peace.[1]

Taking care of yourself also means setting boundaries and saying no to people or situations that cause you excess stress. And as Dr. Pooja Lakshmin reminds us in her book *Real Self-Care*,[2] you don't have to answer your phone.

Similar to how in a plane you're told to put on your oxygen mask before you put on your child's, if you take care of yourself, you can be there for your loved ones.

When you have a young child, finding time for self-care can be hard or even impossible. It may look like getting a quick shower, a short nap, talking to a friend, playing video games like Stardew Valley, or watching HGTV in the middle of the night, when you're up feeding your baby.

Start small, taking a few minutes each day to do something that's for you, even if it's just lying down on the couch and taking in some deep breaths. Every little bit helps.

I like this suggestion from Emily Silver, a parent educator and infant nurse, as described in Corinne Crossley's book, *Self-Care for New Moms.*[3]

The idea is to wake up in the morning and say out loud one thing that you're going to do that day, one thing you aren't going to do, and one thing that you're going to ask for help with. These can be small things.

"I'm going to take a stroller walk with my baby. I'm not going to do the dishes. I'm going to ask a friend or relative to bring over dinner."

Taking part in self-care activities helps us feel less stressed, more confident and energized, and better able to cope with anxiety, depression, and other mental health concerns.[4] When parents take much-needed breaks, they can return to their children calmer and more patient.

> *What self-care looks like will depend on the person and can change over time.*

Look through the following ideas and see which self-care activities you're already doing, or may be interested in trying.[5]

Self-Care Activities

What are your current self-care practices? Is there an area of your life that could use more care?

What's making it hard for you to give yourself the care that you need? What can be done to make it easier? What do you need right now?

Self-Care Activities

Honor yourself

Journal
Practice gratitude
Meditate or pray
Write down five of your strengths
Cross an item off your bucket list
Do something you loved to do as
 a child, like blowing bubbles
Say "no" to something you don't
 want to do
Eat a good meal
Cook your favorite dish

Spend time in nature

Go camping
Get some sun
Go to a park
Have a picnic
Watch a sunrise or sunset
Look up at the stars
Garden

Explore and create

Do a puzzle
Go for a drive
Take photos
Visit a museum
Play an instrument
Play a new boardgame
Visit a landmark you've
 never been to
Do karaoke

Move your body

Stretch
Go for a walk
Do Pilates or yoga
Dance in your living
 room or kitchen
Go for a bike ride
Exercise

Relax your body and mind

Take a nap
Soak in a bath
Read a good book
Use a relaxation app
Take a mental health day
Do breathing exercises
Take a break from
 social media
Have a cup of tea
Use essential oils
Book a massage
Do a face mask
Color

Connect with others

Go on a date
Seek out therapy
Start a game night
Call a friend or loved one
Go to a local Meetup group,
 like knitting or pickleball

It's Not Selfish to Take Time for Yourself

Self-care is not the same thing as being selfish. When people are selfish, they take from others and don't give back.[6] Self-care is about replenishing your resources and finding time to do the things that make you feel better physically, mentally, and emotionally.

You're helping yourself be healthy, so that you can be there for your family, and because you deserve to be cared for, just like your children do. Self-care is an important part of staying healthy and when we do it, we show our kids that they too deserve to take breaks from school and work, to live a happy, well-rounded life.

 Sit and Think: What does self-care look like for you right now? Is there an area in which you would benefit from more self-care?

 Action: Try one or two new self-care activities, no matter how small. How did it go?

 Share: Share your experiences with self-care on your socials with #ParentingWithSelfCompassion or at DrJenFerris.com.

Final Thoughts

"Cut yourself some slack...remember to take care of yourself, get rest whenever you can, and seek support if you need it. And above all, know that you're doing an incredible job, even if it doesn't always feel that way."

Raven Sun

I'm picturing you at the store or at home and your child does not want to leave. You're mindful of the moment and honest about how you're feeling. "This is really hard right now." You see that many people feel this way and you're not alone.

You choose self-kindness. You say to yourself, "I will get through this. What I'm feeling right now is okay. I love my child." And when you speak to yourself this way, you're more likely to treat your child in a gentler way too.

It is possible to be a good parent and to have compassion for yourself. In fact, I might argue that when you have self-compassion, it makes you a better parent.

In this book, we covered topics ranging from infants through pre-teens, including offering choices, picking and choosing your battles, and letting the small stuff go. We talked about the importance of seeing things from your child's point of view and having empathy, being an active listener, using I-messages, applying natural and logical consequences, and taking a parent time-out. We discussed electronics and ways to introduce them into your household. Finally, we considered why self-care is important.

My hope is that you've found some ways to add self-compassion to your life, because I know that you're deserving of kindness and care. The long-term goal is to raise happy, healthy children who, as adults, can take care of themselves, be kind to others, contribute to society, and continue to have a good relationship with you.

Thank you for reading this book. I wish you all the best as you experience the wild but wonderful seas of parenthood.

If you ever want to reach out, you can find me at
DrJenFerris.com.

Bonus

More on Play

"Play is the work of childhood."

Jean Piaget

All over the world, children play. In Article 31 of the United Nations' Convention on the Rights of the Child, they write that children have the right to play and to rest.[1]

Through play, children improve their brain development, act out adult roles, learn social skills, curiosity, confidence, how to work together, and solve problems. Kids get practice in communicating and expressing themselves.

And when we play with our kids, we connect with them and show them that we care.[2]

Infants

When you have a baby in your arms and you swing them around, or when you pretend it's an airplane or a train that's feeding your child, complete with sounds, you and your child are taking part in play.

Play ideas for young infants include mobiles, rattles, and board books. As they get older you can play peekaboo, kick and tickle, this little piggy, and sing songs with hand and body movements like "Twinkle Twinkle Little Star," "The Wheels on the Bus," "The Itsy-Bitsy Spider," and "The Hokey Pokey."

More songs without hand movements for stroller walks and babywearing include "Old MacDonald Had a Farm," "My Girl," "Here Comes the Sun," "I Can See Clearly Now," the chorus to "I Can't Help Myself," and "The ABC song."

You might let your infant bang on a pot with a wooden spoon, finger paint, color with big crayons, and play with funnels and plastic cups in the bathtub.

Toddlers and Preschoolers

Toddlers and preschoolers can play in sand and water, roll a ball back and forth, run around and pop bubbles, play chase, draw with chalk, color with markers, paint with brushes, dress-up and pretend to make dinner, use blocks and puzzles, say "the floor is lava," and have a dance party on a rainy day.

These kids can play hide-and-seek, T-ball, use Play-Doh, play fetch with the dog, have fun with a large cardboard box (playing inside and decorating the outside), and take part in games such as tic-tac-toe, go-fish, and crazy 8s.

On a hot day, you can put your thumb in a hose to make a "'rainbow'" of water and your child can run underneath it in a bathing suit. On a cloudy, windy day, you may want to lie on the grass and see what shapes you can both see in the clouds. Grounding by going barefoot on grass and in nature can connect us to the earth and make us feel happier and less stressed.[3]

School-Age Children

School-age children can play by throwing and catching a ball, doing hopscotch, playing handball, making an obstacle course, hula-hooping, doing arts and crafts like painting rocks, creating paper fans and airplanes, and, with help, making their own tie-dye shirt.

Driving home from school or to an appointment you can try to find a vehicle that matches with each color of the rainbow. On road trips you might play the alphabet game, the "I packed my suitcase" game, or the license plate game. Fun card games now include UNO and Gin Rummy, and you can play board games like Connect 4, Sorry!, and Clue.

Pre-Teens

For pre-teens you can set up a family game night with trivia games, the board game Sequence, and card games like Hearts. You can sing along with them to songs in the car on the way to school. Taylor Swift, anyone?

Game Ideas

Here are some games that I played with my kids.

Bubble forts

When your child is old enough, I'd say around 8, old enough that they won't put their fingers in a fan, they can try building a bubble fort.

You take a king-size sheet, lay it flat on the ground, and put books all around the edges, leaving space for a box fan.

When you turn the fan on the sheet goes up like a big bubble and it becomes a fort in the summertime for kids to go in and read, play games, take a break, and have a snack.

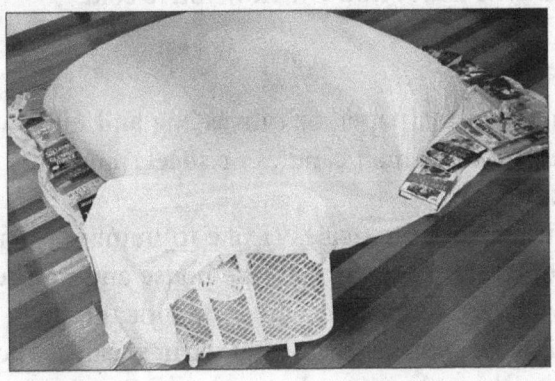

Plastic eggs

After Easter, keep some small plastic eggs to use for this fun activity! Gather ten of them and put small items inside, like stickers, erasers, and small candies.

Then hide them around the house or outside in a safe place, hand out baskets, and get the kids to find all ten. (Maybe the taller child looks for the eggs up high and the shorter kid looks down low. Make sure one child isn't getting too many—it should feel pretty equal.)

Don't put perishable food inside because if you end up not finding one it will start to smell—trust me!

And by counting the number of eggs ahead of time, they know when they're done looking.

If the last one or two are hard to find, you can say, "You're getting warmer. You're hot! Oh, now you're cold."

Treasure hunt

Take one plastic, paper, or canvas bag and fill it with a few little items, such as small candies or snacks and little toys, like matchbox cars.

Then write six to ten clues (I like to number them to keep track) to different places around the house and maybe outside. The kids will need to go away while you hide the clues.

"This is where you get clean." Put the next clue in the bathtub.

"This is where the popsicles are kept." Put the next clue in the freezer.

You hide the bag of toys and treats where the last clue takes them, and you hold onto the first clue to hand to them in person. When your children get older, they can play this game and the egg hunt by themselves, so it's a fun investment.

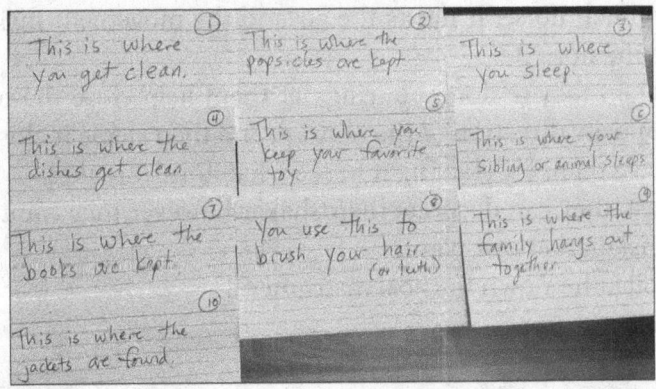

Nature walk

In a safe outdoor space, when the weather is decent, bring paper bags or ziplock bags and go on a nature walk with your child, gathering items from the ground such as dirt, leaves, petals, and grass.

Once you're back at home, your child can glue the items onto construction paper and make a nature collage from the outing.

Music shaker

Save an empty toilet paper roll and staple one side closed.

Have your child pour some uncooked pasta shells, rice, or beans inside to about halfway, not too full. (If it's too full it won't make much noise. It needs the air and the movement inside to create the noise.)

When they're done pouring, let them help close the top in the opposite direction of the bottom, and then staple it closed.

Have them try shaking it to see what noise it makes.

Last, they can decorate their shaker however they want with crayons, markers, or paint.

Voilà, their own musical instrument!

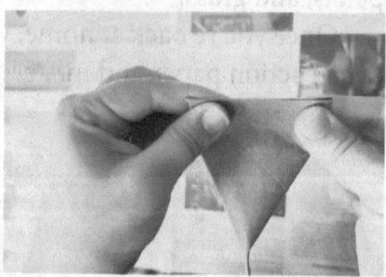

Sit and Think: What games did you like to play as a child? What might your child like to play?

 Action: Try out a new game with your child that they're excited about.

 Share: Share what game you played and how it went on your socials with #ParentingWithSelfCompassion or at DrJenFerris.com.

Bonus

More on Meditation

"All human beings have an innate desire to overcome suffering, to find happiness. Training the mind to think differently, through meditation, is one important way to avoid suffering and be happy."

Dalai Lama

Breathing Meditation

There are meditations that focus on the breath, because breathing is a quick way to come back to the present moment. You can notice how the air feels as you breathe in and out.

Some people like to breathe in and count to five, and then breathe out and count to five.[1]

Senses Meditation

You can meditate on the senses, such as by using the 5-4-3-2-1 technique, where you look for five things you can see, like tiles on the floor; find four things you can touch; three things you hear, such as birds; two things you can smell; and one you can taste. By focusing on your senses it takes you physically back into your body, and can bring about more calm, when you are dealing with anxiety and panic.[2]

Visualization

There is a breath and visualization technique in which you take a breath in and visualize a calm color spreading through you (I like blue or purple). Then you breathe out and imagine a stressful color leaving your body (orange or red for me). While you breathe in and picture your calm color, you can say to yourself, "I breathe in peace and calm." When you breathe out and imagine that color leaving, you can say, "I breathe out stress and anxiety."

I have found this helpful and my college students seemed to enjoy it during midterms. You can also visualize a safe, peaceful place like a warm beach, green forest, birds in the sky, or sunlight streaming into your body.

Walking Meditation

In a walking meditation you can breathe and walk slowly, noticing how it feels as you lift each foot, step, and put it down on the ground. When your mind wanders, bring it back to walking. At the end of the path, take a deep breath, turn around, and walk back.

Body Scan

There are body scan meditations, in which you breathe and scan down your body from your head to your toes, noticing what feels comfortable and what feels uncomfortable. Mental body scans can improve sleep, increase focus, and reduce stress.[3] There's a guided body scan meditation by Kate James on Insight Timer, and there's a free body scan meditation on Headspace.

Grounding Meditation

There are grounding meditations, one in which you close your eyes, breathe, and imagine a large tree with deep roots and a thick trunk. You breathe through the tree and the roots help ground you to the earth.[4]

On Insight Timer there are guided meditations called: "Relieving Anxiety—Feeling Grounded" by Bethany Auriel-Hagan, "Releasing Anxiety" by Kate James, and "Soothing Anxiety" by Andrea Wachter. One guided meditation on grounding and depression is "Healing Session For Depression" by Andrea Wachter.

Loving Kindness Meditation

You can do a loving kindness meditation by closing your eyes, taking some deep breaths, and in your mind, picturing someone you love.

Say silently to yourself, "May you be safe. May you be happy. May you live with ease."

Next, do the same thing with a neutral person, like a cashier, then with a challenging person, such as a family member, and last with all of humanity.

It's also important to do loving kindness meditations with yourself, perhaps picturing yourself as a young child, or as you are now, being hugged by a loved one.

Take a deep breath and think to yourself, "May I be safe. May I be happy. May I live with ease."

You can change the phrases to whatever resonates with you, such as, "May I be kind to myself and others. May I be free of anger. May I feel connected to others."[5] For guided loving kindness meditations you can go to self-compassion.org/self-compassion-practices.

Progressive Muscle Relaxation

Progressive muscle relaxation (PMR) can look like tightening your muscles for five seconds while breathing in, and then relaxing your muscles as you breathe out. Some people like to do this before bed.[6] On Insight Timer, there is a guided PMR meditation by Adam and one by Dr. Marianne Cook.

Sleep Meditation

If you'd like more help with sleep I recommend a guided meditation on Insight Timer by Mary Maddux that's called, "Relax Into Sleep Guided Practice." Other sleep meditations include "Breathing Into Sleep" by Bethany Auriel-Hagan and "Peaceful Sleep" by Kate James.

More information on mindfulness and meditation can be found at Healthy Minds Program, The Mindfulness App, Smiling Mind, Unwinding Anxiety, Petit BamBou, The Breathing App, and Buddhify.

 Sit and Think: Is there any area of your life in which meditation might help? How? Do you have one to three minutes when you wake or at some other point in the day to try meditating? Would you rather take a class in person or online?

 Action: Try a short, silent breath meditation or a guided meditation on a topic of your choosing. What was it like? How did you feel after?

 Share: Share what you selected, when in your day you practiced, and how it went on your socials with #ParentingWithSelfCompassion or at DrJenFerris.com.

About the Author

Dr. Jen Ferris is a writer, former professor of child development, and mother of two. When she's not writing, you'll find her walking, hanging out with her teenagers, or playing with her crazy, sweet dog. She lives in California with her family.

Acknowledgments

I want to thank Dr. Anupama Joshi for being a great mentor, Dr. Marlene Zepeda for teaching me to be concise, and Dr. Ann Bingham-Newman for giving me a chance. Before that there was the late, great Hal Belch who introduced me to child development and psychology, and Mark Bindner who taught me to write what I know.

A big thank you to my incredible editors Kirsten Rees and Liz Pond, and to the beautiful work done by my cover designer Jessica Bell. To my amazing beta readers Dr. Lizzy Tanguay, Donna Agee, and Hilary Ritter, thank you for taking the time and energy to improve this book.

I am grateful to my mom Sandy for the stories, laughter, and for doing better than her parents, to my sister Becca for a supportive place to talk, and to my bonus mom Wendy for the love and enthusiasm. I want to acknowledge Rich and Jan, for their unwavering support and hugs. A big thank you to my dad John for always believing in me, and for teaching me that if you're going to do something, do it well. I hope I did this well.

This book would not be possible without the kind wisdom of Misty Loetterle. Thank you to my fellow writers Hannah and Bryony for listening, giving advice, and reminding me to rest.

To Amanda for being there when I needed you the most, and to Crystal for your feedback, encouragement, and the phrase you left me with after our lunch in the city.

And to Amelie, my first alpha reader and my dear friend. Thank you for the gentle nudges all of these years.

Notes

Chapter 1

1. Glennon Doyle, *Untamed* (The Dial Press, 2020), 85.

2. "What is Self-Compassion?" Self-Compassion, Dr. Kristin Neff, accessed July 5, 2025, https://self-compassion.org/what-is-self-compassion/; Dr. Kristin Neff, *Self-Compassion: The Proven Power of Being Kind to Yourself* (William Morrow Paperbacks, 2015), 51–52, 119, 201, 207, 209, 279.

3. Dr. Christopher K. Germer, *The Mindful Path to Self-Compassion* (The Guilford Press, 2009), 2, 33, 107, 134.

4. Dr. Carla Naumburg, *You Are Not a Sh*tty Parent: How to Practice Self-Compassion and Give Yourself a Break* (Workman Publishing, 2022), 68, 74, 113–114, 142, 181–183; Angela Haupt, "7 Tips for Showing Yourself Some Self-Compassion," *Everyday Health*, July 17, 2023, https://www.everydayhealth.com/emotional-health/tips-for-showing-yourself-some-self-compassion/.

5. Neff, *Self-Compassion*, 51–52, 119, 201, 207, 209, 279; Haupt, "7 Tips."; Sharon Martin, "8 Simple Ways to Increase Self-Compassion," *Psychology Today*, September 8, 2023, https://www.psychologytoday.com/us/blog/conquering-codependency/202306/8-simple-strategies-to-boost-self-compassion; Michelle C. Brooten-Brooks, "What is Self-Compassion? 8 Life-Changing Techniques," *Verywell Health*, June 20, 2024, https://www.verywellhealth.com/self-compassion-5220012; Dr. Susan M. Pollak, *Self-Compassion for Parents: Nurture Your Child by Caring for Yourself* (The Guilford Press, 2019), 26, 41, 107, 176, 219; "Health Benefits of Gratitude," *UCLA Health*, March 22, 2023, https://www.uclahealth.org/news/health-benefits-gratitude.

6. Dr. Pooja Lakshmin, *Real Self-Care: A Transformative Program for Redefining Wellness (Crystals, Cleanses, and Bubble Baths Not Included)* (Penguin Life, 2023), 84, 129, 131.

7. Gill Hasson, *Mindfulness: Live in the Moment. Enjoy Life to the Full* (National Trust, 2019), 21; Dr. Kristen Race, *Mindful Parenting: Simple and Powerful Solutions for Raising Creative, Engaged, Happy Kids in Today's Hectic World* (St. Martin's Griffin, 2013), 22, 148, 155, 160, 166, 174–175, 189–191, 193, 204; Barry Boyce, *The Mindfulness Revolution:*

Leading Psychologists, Scientists, Artists, and Meditation Teachers on the Power of Mindfulness in Daily Life (Shambhala, 2011), 3, 12, 15, 230–234.

8. Hasson, *Mindfulness*, 25.

Chapter 2

1. SWNS, "Myth of the 'Perfect' Parent is Driving Americans Nuts," *New York Post*, September 8, 2017, https://nypost.com/2017/09/08/myth-of-the-perfect-parent-is-driving-americans-nuts/.

2. Tim Senden, "Parents are Too Hard on Themselves: Teens More Positive About Their Parenting," *Medical Xpress*, November 1, 2022, https://medicalxpress.com/news/2022-11-parents-hard-teens-positive-parenting.html.

3. John Pickering, "Today's Parents are Much Too Hard on Themselves," *Washington Post*, January 13, 2015, https://www.washingtonpost.com/posteverything/wp/2015/01/13/todays-parents-are-much-too-hard-on-themselves/.

4. Senden, "Parents."

5. Beth Ellwood, "Young Adults Today are More Perfectionist and Report More Pressure from Their Parents than Previous Generations," *PsyPost*, July 21, 2022, https://www.psypost.org/2022/07/young-adults-today-are-more-perfectionist-and-report-more-pressure-from-their-parents-than-previous-generations-63560.

6. Thomas Curran and Andrew P. Hill, "Perfectionism is increasing over time: A meta-analysis of birth cohort differences from 1989 to 2016," *Psychological Bulletin* 145, 4 (2019): 410–429, https://www.apa.org/pubs/journals/releases/bul-bul0000138.pdf.

7. Kim I. Mills, host, *Speaking of Psychology*, episode 198, "Perfectionism: When Good Enough is Never Good Enough, with Gordon Flett, PhD, and Bonnie Zucker, PsyD," American Psychological Association, July 2022, https://www.apa.org/news/podcasts/speaking-of-psychology/perfectionism.

8. "Perfectionism," APA Dictionary of Psychology, American Psychological Association, last modified April 19, 2018, https://dictionary.apa.org/perfectionism.

9. Brené Brown, *The Gifts of Imperfection: Let Go of Who You Think You're Supposed to Be and Embrace Who You Are* (Hazelden, 2010), 56–57.

10. Elizabeth Scott, "Perfectionism: 10 Signs of Perfectionist Traits," *Verywell Mind*, June 17, 2024, https://www.verywellmind.com/signs-you-may-be-a-perfectionist-3145233.

11. Scott, "Perfectionism."; Lisa Van Gemert, *Perfectionism: A Practical Guide to Managing "Never Good Enough"* (Gifted Guru, 2019), 28, 31, 124.

12. American Psychological Association, "Perfectionism."; Dr. Marianne E. Etherson with Verity Pratt, "Why Perfectionism May Lead to Disordered Eating," *Psychology Today*, November 30, 2022, https://www.psychologytoday.com/us/blog/the-costs-perfectionism/202211/why-perfectionism-may-lead-disordered-eating; Erika Krull, "How are Perfectionism and Addiction Connected?" *GoodRX*, July 21, 2021, https://www.goodrx.com/conditions/substance-use-disorder/perfectionism-and-addiction; Tyler Pia, Igor Galynker, Allison Schuck, Courtney Sinclair, Gelan Ying, and Raffaella Calati, "Perfectionism and Prospective Near-Term Suicidal Thoughts and Behaviors: The Mediation of Fear of Humiliation and Suicide Crisis Syndrome," *International Journal of Environmnetal Research and Public Health* 17, 4 (2020): 1424, https://www.ncbi.nlm.nih.gov/pmc/articles/PMC7068323/

13. David Heitz, "Perfectionism," December 24, 2017, Healthline, https://www.healthline.com/health/perfectionism

14. Van Gemert, "Perfectionism."

15. Meagan Drillinger, "7 Steps to Breaking the 'Perfectionism, Procrastination, Paralysis' Cycle," Healthline, last modified February 24, 2025, https://www.healthline.com/health/anxiety/7-steps-to-breaking-the-perfectionism-procrastination-paralysis-cycle; Elizabeth Scott, "How to Overcome Perfectionism," *Verywell Mind*, April 2, 2024, https://www.verywellmind.com/overcoming-perfectionism-how-to-work-past-perfectionism-3144700.

16. Nancy Colier, "Stop 'Shoulding' Yourself to Death," *Psychology Today*, April 6, 2013, https://www.psychologytoday.com/us/blog/inviting-monkey-tea/201304/stop-shoulding-yourself-death-0.

17. Phyllis Diller, *Phyllis Diller's Housekeeping Hints* (Doubleday, 1966).

Chapter 3

1. George Santayana, *The Life of Reason: Reason in Common Sense* (1905, C. Scribner's Sons), 284.

2. Dr. Lisa Firestone, "Are you Parenting Like Your Parent? For Better or Worse, Many of our Parents' Traits Still Live in Us," *Psychology Today*, November 29, 2012, https://www.psychologytoday.com/us/blog/compassion-matters/201211/are-you-parenting-your-parent.

3. Alexia Roncero, "Childhood Trauma: 3 Steps to Start Healing," *BetterUp*, December 29, 2021, https://www.betterup.com/blog/childhood-trauma.

4. Dr. Sandra Galea and Robert A. Knox, "Trauma and its Aftermath," *Boston University School of Public Health*, July 13, 2018, https://www.bu.edu/sph/news/articles/2018/trauma-and-its-aftermath/.

Chapter 4

1. Michelle Kenney, *Unpunished: How to Let Go of Punishments and Find your Parenting Peace* (MK Publishing, 2023), 73.

2. Raven Sun, *Self-Care for New Moms: First-Time Mothers' Guide to Conquering Postpartum and Finding Joyful Motherhood with Mindfulness Exercises, Self-Care Activities, 100+ Affirmations, and Self-Care Journal* (Raven Sun, 2023), 98–103, 148, 152–153.

3. Sun, *Self-Care*, 98-103, 148, 152-153.

4. Corinne Crossley, *Self-Care for New Moms: Thriving Through your Postpartum Year* (Skyhorse, 2021), 15, 25, 28, 39, 54, 129–130, 176; Dr. Angelica Glover, "5 Reasons Why you Need a Postpartum Support Network," The American College of Obstetricians and Gynecologists, last modified September 2023, https://www.acog.org/womens-health/experts-and-stories/the-latest/5-reasons-why-you-need-a-postpartum-support-network.

5. Jenny Anderson, "What it's Like to Have a Baby in a Country that Actually Cares About New Moms," Quartz, last modified July 21, 2022, https://qz.com/1199605/what-its-like-to-have-a-baby-in-a-country-that-actually-cares-about-new-moms.

6. Glover, "Postpartum Support Network."

7. Zara Abrams, "The Urgent Necessity for Paid Parental Leave," American Psychological Association, April 1, 2022, https://www.apa.org/monitor/2022/04/feature-parental-leave.

8. Dr Jonathan H. Westover, "Supporting new parents: Why organizations should offer both maternity and paternity leave," Human Capital Innovations, February 26, 2024, https://www.innovativehumancapital.com/article/supporting-new-parents-why-organizations-should-offer-both-maternity-and-paternity-leave.

9. Abrams, "Paid Parental Leave."; "Parental Leave Brings Mental Health Benefits, Especially for Mothers," *APA Blogs*, American Psychiatric Association, January 24, 2023, https://www.psychiatry.org/newsroom/apa-blogs/parental-leave-mental-health-benefits; David Walsh, "Finland Named the World's Happiest Country (Again) in 2024 but Young People in Europe are Struggling", *Euro News*, March 20, 2024, https://www.euronews.com/health/2024/03/20/finland-named-the-

worlds-happiest-country-again-in-2024-but-young-people-in-europe-are-str.

10. Abrams, "Paid Parental Leave."; Anders Chronholm, "Fathers' Experience of Shared Parental Leave in Sweden," *Recherches Sociologiques et Anthropologiques* 38, 2 (2007): 9–25, https://journals.openedition.org/rsa/456?lang=en.

11. Abrams, "Paid Parental Leave."

12. Walsh, "World's happiest country."; Kelsey Rolfe, "A Closer Look at Finland's New Flexible Parental Leave," Benefits Canada, August 9, 2024, https://www.benefitscanada.com/archives_/benefits-canada-archive/a-closer-look-at-finlands-new-flexible-parental-leave/.

13. Glover, "Postpartum Support Network."

14. Glover, "Postpartum Support Network."

15. Michelle D. Hardy, "The Role and Scope of the Postpartum Doula," International Childbirth Education Association, July 2017, https://icea.org/wp-content/uploads/2015/12/Role-Scope-of-Postpartum-Doula-3.pdf.

16. "Postpartum Doula," American Pregnancy Association, accessed July 6, 2025, https://americanpregnancy.org/healthy-pregnancy/planning/postpartum-doula/.

17. "How to Hire a Doula," DONA International, accessed July 6, 2025, https://www.dona.org/what-is-a-doula-2/how-to-hire-a-doula/.

18. "La Leche League meetings," La Leche League International, February 2020, https://llli.org/la-leche-league-meetings/.

19. Jada Shapiro, "How to Choose a Lactation Consultant," Babylist, last modified May 15, 2025, https://www.babylist.com/hello-baby/how-to-choose-lactation-consultant

20. Deepi Brar, "How to Find the Best Mom Groups Near You," *Babycenter*, August 28, 2023, https://www.babycenter.com/family/motherhood/joining-a-moms-group-how-to-find-one-that-suits-you_11800.

21. "How to Choose a Psychologist," American Psychological Association, Occtober 17, 2019, https://www.apa.org/topics/psychotherapy/choose-therapist; Gloria Oladipo, "How to Find the Right Therapist: 10 Tips," *PsychCentral*, last modified March 5, 2025, https://psychcentral.com/blog/10-ways-to-find-a-good-therapist#therapy-type.

Chapter 5

1. Deborah Carlisle Solomon, *Baby Knows Best: Raising a Confident and Resourceful Child, the RIE Way* (Little, Brown and Company, 2013), 29, 192, 201–203, 205.

2. Amanda Russo, "Telling our kids 'Don't do that' and 'Stop' doesn't work," *Scary Mommy*, December 5, 2019, https://www.scarymommy.com/change-behavior-approach.

3. Elizabeth Pantley, *The No-Cry Discipline Solution: Gentle Ways to Encourage Good Behavior, Without Whining, Tantrums, and Tears* (McGraw Hill, 2007), 71–72, 84, 112.

4. Rebecca Eanes, "Your Words Affect Your Child's Brain," *Generation Mindful*, accessed July 6, 2025, https://genmindful.com/blogs/mindful-moments/your-words-affect-your-child-s-brain.

5. Magda Gerber and Allison Johnson, *Your Self-Confident Baby: How to Encourage Your Child's Natural Abilities—From the Very Start* (John Wiley & Sons, 1998), 29–30, 95–96, 99, 139, 211.

Chapter 6

1. Dr. Erin Leyba, "5 Guidelines for Giving Kids Choices," *Psychology Today*, February 1, 2016, https://www.psychologytoday.com/us/blog/joyful-parenting/201602/5-guidelines-giving-kids-choices; Dr. Allie Ticktin, "6 Powerful Benefits of Giving your Child a Choice," *Motherly*, last modified February 15, 2025, https://www.mother.ly/child/benefits-of-giving-child-choices/; Alfie Kohn, *Unconditional Parenting: Moving from Rewards and Punishments to Love and Reason* (Atria, 2005), 63, 67–68, 157.

2. Suzanne Zuckerman, "5 Battles you Shouldn't Bother Fighting with your Kid—And 4 you Should Fight to Win," *PureWow*, February 20, 2020, https://www.purewow.com/family/kid-refuses-to-wear-coat-parenting-battles.

3. Ticktin, "Giving your Child a Choice."

4. Dr. Erin Leyba, "Giving Kids Choices."

5. Carlisle Solomon, *Baby Knows Best*, 29, 192, 201–203, 205.

6. Ticktin, "Giving your Child a Choice."

7. Pantley, *The No-Cry Discipline Solution*, 71–72, 84, 112; Carlisle Solomon, *Baby Knows Best*, 29, 192, 201–203, 205; Susie Allen, "Are you Offering your Children Too Many Choices?" *Kellog Insight*, September 5, 2017, https://insight.kellogg.northwestern.edu/article/choice-set-size-and-children; Kohn, *Unconditional Parenting*, 63, 67-68, 157.

Chapter 7

1. Suzanne Zuckerman, "5 Battles you Shouldn't Bother Fighting with your Kid—And 4 you Should Fight to Win," *PureWow*, February 20, 2020, https://www.purewow.com/family/kid-refuses-to-wear-coat-parenting-battles.

Chapter 8

1. Gabbi Shaw, "A Scientific Study Claims that your Age Affects How you See this Famous Optical Illusion," *Business Insider*, June 30, 2020, https://www.businessinsider.com/study-says-age-affects-optical-illusion-2018-9.

2. Kathleen S. Berger, *The Developing Person: Through Childhood and Adolescence* (Worth, 2018a), 252; Robert S. Feldman, *Child Development: A Topical Approach* (Pearson, 2014), 172, 383; Max-Planck-Gesellschaft, "Outgrowing Emotional Egocentricity: Linked Brain Region Discovered," *Science Daily*, May 27, 2014, www.sciencedaily.com/releases/2014/05/140527101456.htm.

3. Ashley Patek, "Our Children may be Self-Centered, but they Aren't Selfish," *Generation Mindful*, accessed July 6, 2025, https://genmindful.com/blogs/mindful-moments/our-children-may-be-self-centered-but-they-arent-selfish.

4. Patek, 2023, "Our Children Aren't Selfish."

5. Lori Deschene, "Tiny Wisdom: Treat People How they Want to be Treated," Tiny Buddha, accessed July 6, 2025, https://tinybuddha.com/quotes/tiny-wisdom-treat-people-how-they-want-to-be-treated/; Dr. Barry M. Prizant, *Uniquely Human: A Different Way of Seeing Autism* (Simon and Schuster, 2015), 17, 31, 138, 140, 151, 264; Rebecca Parlakian, "How to Help your Child Develop Empathy," Zero to Three, February 1, 2016, https://www.zerotothree.org/resource/how-to-help-your-child-develop-empathy/.

6. Stuart Passmore, "Why Empathy is Important in Parenting," Welldoing, May 10, 2016, https://welldoing.org/article/why-empathy-important-parenting-child.

7. Dr. Judith Orloff, *The Genius of Empathy: Practical Skills to Heal your Sensitive Self, your Relationships & the World* (Sounds True, 2024), 40–43, 53–54, 64, 67, 122, 207.

8. Thu-Huong Ha, "5 Exercises to Help You Build More Empathy," Ideas. TED.com, March 16, 2021, https://ideas.ted.com/5-exercises-to-help-you-build-more-empathy/.

9. Kristen Rogers, "Empathy is Both a Trait and a Skill. Here is How to Strengthen it," *CNN*, June 24, 2020, https://www.cnn.com/2020/06/24/health/develop-empathy-skills-wellness/index.html.

10. Passmore, "Why Empathy is Important."

11. Cathy Cassani Adams, *Zen Parenting: Caring for Ourselves and our Children in an Unpredictable World* (Hachette Go books, 2022), 127; Claire Cain Miller, "How to be More Empathetic," *The New York Times*, December 1, 2018, https://www.nytimes.com/guides/year-of-living-better/how-to-be-more-empathetic; Dr. John Gottman and Joan Declaire, *Raising an Emotionally Intelligent Child* (Fireside, 1997), 24, 94, 99–100, 104–105, 123; "5 Tips for Cultivating Empathy," Harvard Graduate School of Education, last modified March 2021, https://mcc.gse.harvard.edu/resources-for-families/5-tips-cultivating-empathy.

12. "Empathy Quiz," *Greater Good Magazine*, Greater Good Science Center at University of California, Berkeley, accessed July 7, 2025, https://greatergood.berkeley.edu/quizzes/take_quiz/empathy.

Chapter 9

1. "Communicating Well with Babies and Children: Tips," Raising Children Network, last modified July 4, 2023, https://raisingchildren.net.au/toddlers/connecting-communicating/communicating/communicating-well-with-children; Kristen Zolten and Dr. Nicholas Long, "Parent/Child Communication," Center for Effective Parenting, 2006, https://parenting-ed.org/wp-content/themes/parenting-ed/files/handouts/communication-parent-to-child.pdf.

2. "Why Active Listening is Important in Parent–Child Relationships," The Family Centre, March 1, 2022, https://www.familycentre.org/news/post/why-active-listening-is-important-in-parent-child-relationships.

3. "Top 11 Skills Employers Look for in Job Candidates," Indeed, last modified January 29, 2025, https://www.indeed.com/career-advice/resumes-cover-letters/skills-employers-look-for.

4. The Family Centre, "Active Listening."

5. Arlin Cuncic, "7 Active Listening Techniques for Better Communication," *Verywell Mind*, last modified February 12, 2024, https://www.verywellmind.com/what-is-active-listening-3024343; The Family Centre, "Active Listening".

6. Erin Johnston, "What are 'I Feel' Statements?" *Verywell Mind,* last modified November 25, 2023, https://www.verywellmind.com/what-are-feeling-statements-425163; "'I' Message," *GoodTherapy,* last modified February 14, 2018, https://www.goodtherapy.org/blog/psychpedia/i-message.

7. Johnston, "'I Feel' Statements".

8. "5 Benefits of Sportscasting our Child's Struggles," Janet Lansbury, accessed July 7, 2025, https://www.janetlansbury.com/2013/04/5-benefits-of-sportscasting-your-childs-struggles.

9. Dr. Michele Borba, *Unselfie: Why Empathetic Kids Succeed in our All-About-Me World* (Touchstone, 2016), 17, 69, 159, 188–189.

10. Carlisle Solomon, *Baby Knows Best,* 29, 192, 201–203, 205; Raising Children Network, "Communicating Well."; Janet Lansbury, *No Bad Kids: Toddler Discipline Without Shame* (JLML Press, 2014), 21, 45, 106, 121.

11. Emily Kircher-Morris, *Raising Twice-Exceptional Children: A Handbook for Parents of Neurodivergent Gifted Kids,* (Routledge, 2022), 11, 41–42, 101–102, 121, 173–174.

12. Prizant, *Uniquely Human,* 17, 31, 138, 140, 151, 264.

13. Dr. Odelya Gertel Kraybill, "Parenting a Neurodivergent Child is Hard! Self-Compassion is the Antidote to Stress and Pain," *Psychology Today,* August 1, 2021, https://www.psychologytoday.com/us/blog/expressive-trauma-integration/202108/parenting-neurodivergent-child-is-hard.

14. Prizant, *Uniquely Human,* 17, 31, 138, 140, 151, 264; Dr. Sharon Saline, *What your ADHD Child Wishes You Knew: Working Together to Empower Kids for Success in School and Life* (TarcherPerigee Books, 2018), 24, 128, 173; Kircher-Morris, *Raising Twice-Exceptional Children,* 11, 41–42, 101–102, 121, 173–174; Audra Mills, *The Art of Parenting a Child with Autism and Asperger's: Meet their Unique Needs, See the World Through their Eyes, and Unlock their Full Potential* (2023), 58, 63, 66, 69–70, 75–76, 79, 82, 98, 103, 130, 133–134, 154; Dr. Russell A. Barkley, *12 Principles for Raising a Child with ADHD* (The Guilford Press, 2021), 57, 92, 103, 120, 151, 170; Tony Attwood, *The Complete Guide to Asperger's Syndrome* (Jessica Kingsley, 2007), 78, 93–94.

Chapter 10

1. Ken Ginsburg, "What does Discipline Really Mean?" Center for Parent & Teen Communication, February 4, 2025, https://parentandteen.com/what-does-discipline-really-mean/.

2. Alfie Kohn, *Unconditional Parenting: Moving from Rewards and Punishments to Love and Reason*, (Atria, 2005), 63, 67–68, 157; Alfie Kohn, *Punished by Rewards: The Trouble with Gold Stars, Incentive Plans, A's, Praise, and Other Bribes* (Houghton Mifflin, 1999), 76, 78, 92–93, 166–167, 170.

3. Hunter Clarke-Fields, *Raising Good Humans: A Mindful Guide to Breaking the Cycle of Reactive Parenting and Raising Kind, Confident Kids* (New Harbinger, 2019), 16–17, 47, 83, 126–129, 145.

4. Kohn, *Unconditional Parenting*, 63, 67–68, 157.

5. "AAP says spanking harms children," American Academy of Pediatrics, November 5, 2018, https://www.aap.org/en/news-room/news-releases/aap/2018/aap-says-spanking-harms-children/.

6. Christina Caron, "Spanking is Ineffective and Harmful to Children, Pediatricians' Group Says," *The New York Times*, November 5, 2018, https://www.nytimes.com/2018/11/05/health/spanking-harmful-study-pediatricians.html.

7. "Should You Spank your Child?" Peaceful Parent, Happy Kids, Dr. Laura Markham, accessed July 7, 2025, https://www.peacefulparenthappykids.com/read/should-I-spank-my-child.

8. Dr. Saul McLeod, "Bandura's Bobo Doll Experiment on Social Learning," *Simply Psychology*, May 19, 2025, https://www.simplypsychology.org/bobo-doll.html.

9. Claire Gillespie, "Timeouts are a Dated and Ineffective Parenting Strategy. So What's a Good Alternative?" *The Washington Post*, November 19, 2018, https://www.washingtonpost.com/lifestyle/2018/11/19/timeouts-are-dated-ineffective-parenting-strategy-so-whats-good-alternative/.

10. "What's Wrong with Timeouts?" Peaceful Parent, Happy Kids, Dr. Laura Markham, accessed July 7, 2025, https://www.peacefulparenthappykids.com/read/timeouts; Judy Arnall, "Why Timeout as a Punishment Doesn't Work," The Attached Family, March 2, 2010, http://theattachedfamily.com/membersonly/?p=2455.

11. Kohn, *Punished by Rewards*, 76, 78, 92–93, 166–167, 170.

12. Kohn, *Unconditional Parenting*, 63, 67–68, 157.

13. Dr. Laura Markham, "Being Hard on Yourself Doesn't Make You a Better Parent," *Psychology Today*, September 13, 2017, https://www.psychologytoday.com/us/blog/peaceful-parents-happy-kids/201709/being-hard-yourself-doesnt-make-you-better-parent.

14. Dr. Becky A. Bailey, *Easy to Love, Difficult To Discipline: The 7 Basic Skills for Turning Conflict into Cooperation* (William Morrow, 2001), 101, 173, 198–199.

15. Dr. Jane Nelsen, "Logical Consequences," Positive Discipline, accessed July 7, 2025, https://www.positivediscipline.com/articles/logical-consequences.

16. "What is the 5 by 5 Rule and How to Use It," Alexander Cameron, accessed July 7, 2025, https://www.alexandercameron.ca/single-post/2018/11/01/what-is-the-5-by-5-rule-and-how-to-use-it-reading-time-4-minutes.

17. Jill Ceder, "Why a Consistent Approach to your Parenting is Important," *ParentCo.*, January 9, 2018, https://www.parent.com/blogs/conversations/2018-why-a-consistent-approach-to-your-parenting-is-important.

18. Clarke-Fields, *Raising Good Humans*, 16-17, 47, 83, 126–129, 145.

19. Teri Mahoney, "Using Humor in your Home," The Center for Parenting Education, accessed July 7, 2025, https://centerforparentingeducation.org/library-of-articles/healthy-communication/using-humor-home/; "Using Humor as a Parenting Tool," Michelle Grosser, accessed July 7, 2025, https://michellegrosser.com/2022/05/30/humor/.

20. Prizant, *Uniquely Human*, 17, 31, 138, 140, 151, 264; Saline, *What your ADHD Child Wishes You Knew*, 24, 128, 173; Kircher-Morris, *Raising Twice-Exceptional Children*, 11, 41–42, 101–102, 121, 173–174; Mills, *The Art of Parenting a Child with Autism and Asperger's*, 58, 63, 66, 69–70, 75–76, 79, 82, 98, 103, 130, 133–134, 154; Barkley, *12 Principles for Raising a Child with ADHD*, 57, 92, 103, 120, 151, 170.

Chapter 11

1. Jennifer Korn and Marie Barbier, "A Look Back at Every iPhone Ever," *CNN*, September 11, 2023, https://www.cnn.com/2023/09/11/tech/iphone-timeline/index.html.

2. Bharti Adhikari, "Advantages and Disadvantages of Letting Your Child Use Too Much of Electronic Gadgets," *Parent Circle*, accessed July 7, 2025, https://www.parentcircle.com/advantages-disadvantages-of-electronic-gadgets-for-students/article; Anya Kamenetz, *The Art of Screen Time: Digital Parenting Without Fear* (Hachette, 2018), 22–24, 39, 59–60.

3. Sarah Berger, "Tech-Free Dinners and No Smart Phones Past 10pm—How Steve Jobs, Bill Gates and Mark Cuban Limited Their Kids' Screen Time," Make It, *CNBC*, June 5, 2018, https://www.cnbc.com/2018/06/05/how-bill-gates-mark-cuban-and-others-limit-their-kids-tech-use.html; Andrea Nelson, "How Tech CEOs and Founders Manage their Kids'

Screen Time," *Bright Canary*, March 14, 2024, https://www.brightcanary. io/tech-ceos-screen-time-for-kids/.

4. Dr. Natasha Burgery, "What is the Best Age for a Child's First Smartphone?" *Forbes*, October 9, 2023, https://www.forbes.com/health/ family/best-age-for-first-cell-phone/.

5. Carolanne Bamford-Beattie, "How Can I Detox my Children from their Screens?" February 1, 2022, https://kidslox.com/how-to/detox-your-child-from-electronics/.

6. Bamford-Beattie, "Detox Children from Screens."

7. Edward Luker, "Are Video Games, Screens Another Addiction?" Mayo Clinic Health System, July 1, 2022, https://www.mayoclinichealthsystem. org/hometown-health/speaking-of-health/are-video-games-and-screens-another-addiction; Kamenetz, *The Art of Screen Time*, 22–24, 39, 59–60; Dr. Richard Freed, *Wired Child: Reclaiming Childhood in a Digital Age* (CreateSpace, 2015), 21, 52–53, 78; Johann Hari, *Stolen Focus: Why you Can't Pay Attention—and How To Think Deeply Again* (Crown, 2022), 40, 106, 115, 243.

8. Kamenetz, *The Art of Screen Time*, 22–24, 39, 59–60; Freed, *Wired Child*, 21, 52–53, 78; Dr. Mike Brooks and Dr. Jon Lasser, *Tech Generation: Raising Balanced Kids in a Hyper-Connected World* (Oxford University Press, 2018), 138–140, 165, 181.

9. "Beyond Screen Time: Help your Kids Build Healthy Media Use Habits," Healthy Children, American Academy of Pediatrics, last modified July 20, 2022, https://www.healthychildren.org/English/family-life/ Media/Pages/healthy-digital-media-use-habits-for-babies-toddlers-preschoolers.aspx; Hailey Middlebrook, "New Screen Time Rules for Kids, by Doctors," *CNN*, October 21, 2016, https://www.cnn. com/2016/10/21/health/screen-time-media-rules-children-aap/.

10. Heather Kelly, "What Age Should You Give a Kid their First Phone?" *The Washington Post*, September 7, 2023, https://www.washingtonpost.com/ technology/2023/what-age-kid-phone/

11. Brooks and Lasser, *Tech Generation*, 138–140, 165, 181; Dr. Devorah Heitner, *Screenwise: Helping Kids Thrive (and Survive) in their Digital World* (Bibliomotion, 2016), 70–71, 112, 171–172; Diana Graber, *Raising Humans in a Digital World: Helping Kids Build a Healthy Relationship with Technology* (HarperCollins, 2019), 85, 91, 98, 116, 123–124.

12. Avery Elizabeth Hurt, "Will You Learn Better from Reading on Screen or on Paper?" *Science News Explores*, October 18, 2021, https://www. snexplores.org/article/learn-comprehension-reading-digital-screen-paper; Kerry Benson, "Reading on Paper Versus Screens: What's the Difference?" *Brain Facts*, July 28, 2020, https://www.brainfacts.org/

neuroscience-in-society/tech-and-the-brain/2020/reading-on-paper-versus-screens-whats-the-difference-072820.

13. Hurt, "Reading on Screen or on Paper."

14. Hurt, "Reading on Screen or on Paper."

15. Gill Hasson, *Mindfulness*, 21, 25; Dr. Kristen Race, Mindful Parenting, 22, 148, 155, 160, 166, 174–175, 189–191, 193, 204; Barry Boyce, *The Mindfulness Revolution: Leading Psychologists, Scientists, Artists, and Meditation Teachers on the Power of Mindfulness in Daily Life* (Shambhala, 2011), 3, 12, 15, 230–234.

16. Tracy E. McDowell, "What is Digital Mindfulness?" *Medium*, February 23, 2023, https://medium.com/@tracymcdowell/what-is-digital-mindfulness-f246acffd948.

17. Jake Knapp and John Zeratski, *Make Time: How to Focus on What Matters Every Day* (Currency, 2018), 95, 115.

Chapter 12

1. Angela Cabotaje, "What does Self-Care Mean – and Why is it Important?" *Right as Rain by UW Medicine*, December 30, 2020, https://rightasrain.uwmedicine.org/mind/mental-health/self-care-meaning; Nicole Goodman and Lauren Mishcon, *Have you Tried This? The Only Self Care Guide you will Ever Need* (Welbeck Balance, 2024), 8, 107, 155, 163.

2. Dr. Pooja Lakshmin, *Real Self-Care: A Transformative Program for Redefining Wellness (Crystals, Cleanses, and Bubble Baths Not Included)* (Penguin Life, 2023), 84, 129, 131.

3. Corinne Crossley, *Self-Care for New Moms: Thriving Through your Postpartum Year* (Skyhorse, 2021), 15, 25, 28, 39, 54, 129–130, 176.

4. Cabotaje, "What does Self-Care Mean?"; Rachel Ann Tee-Melegrito, "What are Examples of Self-Care?" *Medical News Today*, last modified March 28, 2023, https://www.medicalnewstoday.com/articles/self-care-examples.

5. Raven Sun, *Self-Care for New Moms: First-Time Mothers' Guide to Conquering Postpartum and Finding Joyful Motherhood with Mindfulness Exercises, Self-Care Activities, 100+ Affirmations, and Self-Care Journal* (Raven Sun, 2023), 98–103, 148, 152–153; Beccy Hands and Alexis Stickland, *The Little Book of Self-Care for New Mums* (Vermilion, 2018), 32–33, 74, 79, 86, 100, 105, 116; Dr. Kristen Race, *Mindful Parenting*, 22, 148, 155, 160, 166, 174–175, 189–191, 193, 204; Goodman and Mishcon, *Have you Tried This?* 8, 107, 155, 163; Dr. Emily Guarnatta,

"99 Self-Care Activities You Can Try Right Now," *GoodRX*, August 8, 2023, https://www.goodrx.com/health-topic/mental-health/self-care-ideas-activities; Tee-Melegrito, "Examples of Self-Care."; Ivy Conrad, "Benefits of Massage Therapy," Mayo Clinic Health System, March 22, 2022, https://www.mayoclinichealthsystem.org/hometown-health/speaking-of-health/benefits-of-massage-therapy.

6. Rebekah Lee, "Is Self-Care, Selfish?" Morson Talent, May 1, 2022, https://www.morson.com/is-self-care-selfish.

Bonus: More on Play

1. "Convention on the Rights of the Child," Human Rights Instruments, *United Nations,* November 20, 1989, https://www.ohchr.org/en/instruments-mechanisms/instruments/convention-rights-child.

2. Clarke-Fields, *Raising Good Humans,* 16–17, 47, 83, 126–129, 145.; "How Play Helps Children's Development," *NIDirect*, accessed July 7, 2025, https://www.nidirect.gov.uk/articles/how-play-helps-childrens-development; "Importance of Play in Early Childhood," Head Start, last modified April 21, 2024, https://eclkc.ohs.acf.hhs.gov/curriculum/article/importance-play-early-childhood.

3. Eleesha Lockett, "Grounding: Can Walking Barefoot on the Earth Heal You?" Healthline, last modified February 28, 2025, https://www.healthline.com/health/grounding.

Bonus: More on Meditation

1. Naumburg, *You Are Not a Sh*tty Parent*, 68, 74, 113–114, 142, 181–183; Race, *Mindful Parenting*, 22, 148, 155, 160, 166, 174–175, 189–191, 193, 204.

2. Naumburg, *You Are Not a Sh*tty Parent*, 68, 74, 113–114, 142, 181–183; Goodman and Mishcon, *Have you Tried This?* 8, 107, 155, 163.

3. Shonda Moralis, *Breathe, Mama, Breathe: 5-Minute Mindfulness for Busy Moms* (The Experiment, 2017), 4, 42, 74, 258; Crystal Raypole, "How to do a Body Scan Meditation (and Why you Should)," Healthline, December 5, 2022, https://www.healthline.com/health/body-scan-meditation; Dr. Elizabeth Scott, "What is Body Scan Meditation?" *Verywell Mind*, last modified February 12, 2024, https://www.verywellmind.com/body-scan-meditation-why-and-how-3144782; "Body Scan Meditation to Reduce Stress," *Headspace*, accessed July 7, 2025, https://www.headspace.com/meditation/body-scan.

4. "Tree Grounding Meditation," *Treecreate*, May 6, 2021, https://treecreate. org/2021/05/06/tree-grounding-meditation/; Joanne Lee, "Grounding with Tree Roots," *Insight Timer* (audio), accessed July 7, 2025, https:// insighttimer.com/joanneleelifecoach/guided-meditations/grounding-with-tree-root

5. Dr. Kristin Neff, *Self-Compassion: The Proven Power of Being Kind to Yourself* (William Morrow Paperbacks, 2015), 51–52, 119, 201, 207, 209, 279; Dr. Christopher K. Germer, *The Mindful Path to Self-Compassion* (The Guilford Press, 2009), 2, 33, 107, 134.; Naumburg, *You Are Not a Sh*tty Parent*, 68, 74, 113–114, 142, 181–183.

6. Moralis, *Breathe, Mama, Breathe*, 4, 42, 74, 258.